New Mexico Dreamscapes II

Bobby J. Jones

New Mexico Dreamscapes II

Copyright © 2018 Bobby J. Jones

All rights reserved.

ISBN:13:9781987652741.
ISBN-10:1987652746.

DEDICATION

I dedicate New Mexico Dreamscapes II and its beautiful images to the loving memory of my maternal grandmother Sue Morrison Brown. Texas Technological College Class of 1932.

New Mexico Dreamscapes II

Table of Contents

Acknowledgment...Page 10

Image 1..Page 13

Image 2..Page 15

Image 3..Page 17

Image 4..Page 19

Image 5..Page 21

Image 6..Page 23

Image 7..Page 25

Image 8..Page 27

Image 9..Page 29

Image 10..Page 31

Image 11..Page 33

Image 12..Page 35

Image 13..Page 37

Image 14..Page 39

Image 15..Page 41

Image 16..Page 43

Image 17..Page 45

Image 18..Page 47

Image 19..Page 49

Image 20..Page 51

Image 21..Page 53

Image 22..Page 55

Image 23..Page 57

Image 24..Page 59

Image 25	Page 61
Image 26	Page 63
Image 27	Page 65
Image 28	Page 67
Image 29	Page 69
Image 30	Page 71
Image 31	Page 73
Image 32	Page 75
Image 33	Page 77
Image 34	Page 79
Image 35	Page 81
Image 36	Page 83
Image 37	Page 85
Image 38	Page 87
Image 39	Page 89
Image 40	Page 91
Image 41	Page 93
Image 42	Page 95
Image 43	Page 97
Image 44	Page 99
Image 45	Page 101
Image 46	Page 103
Image 47	Page 105
Image 48	Page 107
Image 49	Page 109
Image 50	Page 111
Image 51	Page 113

Image 52......Page 115

Image 53......Page 117

Image 54......Page 119

Image 55......Page 121

Image 56......Page 123

Image 57......Page 125

Image 58......Page 127

Image 59......Page 129

Image 60......Page 131

Image 61......Page 133

About the Author......Page 135

New Mexico Dreamscapes II

ACKNOWLEGMENT

BOBBY J. JONES ACKNOWLEDGES THE MEMORY OF HIS MATERNAL GRANDMOTHER SUE MORRISON BROWN. MRS. BROWN WAS BORN AND RAISED IN CROSBY COUNTY, TEXAS IN 1902. THIS COUNTY IS THE COUNTY EAST OF LUBBOCK, TEXAS. HER PARENTS WERE THOMAS JEFFERSOM MORRISON AND EMMA CLEMENTINE REAGAN. THEY WERE CROSBY COUNTY PIONEERS IN THE 1890S. THEY HAD THREE CHILDREN. THEY INCLUDE CHARLES THOMAS "CHARLEY" MORRISON, SUSANNAH MALISSA "SUE" MORRISON BROWN, AND ALVIN REAGAN "JAKE" MORRISON.

I RECALL MANY FOND STORIES FROM MY MATERNAL GRANDMOTHER. THEY INCLUDE GROWING UP IN TEXAS AT THE BEGINNING OF THE 20TH CENTURY, TEACHING IN CROSBY COUNTY, TEXAS DURING THE 1920S, ATTENDING TEXAS TECHNOLOGICAL COLLEGE (TEXAS TECH UNIVERSITY) DURING THE GREAT DEPRESSION, HOW SHE MET MY MATERNAL GRANDFATHER EDWARD WATTS BROWN, AND STORIES ABOUT MY MOM AND HER SISTERS (HER THREE DAUGHTERS).

WHILE ATTENDING TEXAS TECHNOLOGICAL COLLEGE, MY MATERNAL GRANDMOTHER WAS A HOME ECONOMICS MAJOR (CLOTHING AND TEXTILES). SUE HAD A VERY FINE EYE FOR SEWING AND COULD SEW A MEAN STITCH WITH THE SEWING MACHINE. I RECALL WHEN MY GRANDMOTHER PASSED AWAY IN 1983. MY MOM AND MY AUNTS PILED MY GRANDMOTHER'S CLOTHES ON TOP OF ONE THE GUEST BEDROOM BEDS TO THE CEILING. THESE CLOTHES CONSISTED OF NEARLY 5 DECADES OF FASHIONS THAT MY GRANDMOTHER CREATED ON HER SEWING MACHINES.

AS A CHILD, I SPENT MY SUMMERS WITH MY GRANDMOTHER BROWN ON HER FARM EAST OF REESE AIR FORCE BASE. I REMEMBER WAKING UP IN THE MORNING AND EATING BREAKFAST. WE DROVE INTO TOWN. SHE SHOPPED FOR HER FASHION PATTERNS AND MATERIAL TO CREATE AN OUTFIT IN ONE DAY. WE STOPPED BY THE GROCERY STORE AND SHOPPED FOR OUR FOOD FOR THE NEXT SEVERAL DAYS. WE MADE LUNCH TOGETHER AND AFTERWARDS CREATED HER OUTFIT FOR THE WEEK.

MY GRANDMOTHER PLACE HER PATTERN BOARD ON THE DINING ROOM TABLE, LAID OUT HER MATERIAL, THEN PINNED THE PATTERNS TO THE MATERIAL, AND CUT OUT HER PATTERNS. ABOUT AN HOUR LATER, SHE

SEWN HER PATTERNS TOGETHER. BEFORE DINNER. SHE HAD HER OUTFIT SEWN TOGETHER AND MADE ADJUSTMENTS. AS A CHILD, I WAS VERY IMPRESSED BY HER SEWING ABILITIES. MY GRANDMOTHER AND MY MOM TAUGHT ME HOW TO THREAD A BOBBIN AND A SEWING MACHINE AT AN EARLY AGE. I REMEMBER MY GRANDMOTHER MAKING NEEDLEPOINT IMAGES AND KNITTING IN HER LIVING ROOM IN THE SUMMER EVENING HOURS.

I HAVE BEEN TOLD BY SEVERAL FRIENDS THAT MY IMAGES, I CREATE, REMIND THEM OF NEEDLE POINT. BOTH MY GRANDMOTHER AND MY MOTHER LOVED NEEDLE POINT. THEY CONSTANTLY CREATED NEEDLE POINT WORKS. THE PATTERNS THAT ARE SEEN IN MY ART REMIND ME OF THE PRINTED MATERIAL DESIGNS THAT MY GRANDMOTHER USED TO CREATE HER OUTFITS.

I WOULD ALSO LIKE TO ACKNOWLEDGE MY FRIEND AND COLLEAGUE, MIKE WRIGHT, THE COMPUTER INSTRUCTOR AT ADOBE ACRES ELEMENTARY SCHOOL 2017-2018 SCHOOL YEAR. HE IS A GUIDING FORCE IN MY ART PUBLICTIONS. I APPRECIATE HIS EXPERTISE IN USING THE FORMATS ON CREATESPACE.COM IN CREATING MY PUBLICATIONS FOR AMAZON. THANK YOU, MIKE!

A SPECIAL THANK YOU TO MY MATERNAL GRANDMOTHER SUE MORRISON BROWN! SHE PAVED THE WAY FOR HER CHILDREN, HER GRANDCHILDREN, AND GREAT GRANDCHILDREN TO ATTEND COLLEGE. SHE WAS A GUIDING LIGHT TO ALL THAT KNEW HER AND LOVED HER. I LOVE YOU AND MISS YOU, GRANDMA! YOU CONTINUE TO BE A GUIDING SPIRIT IN MY LIFE

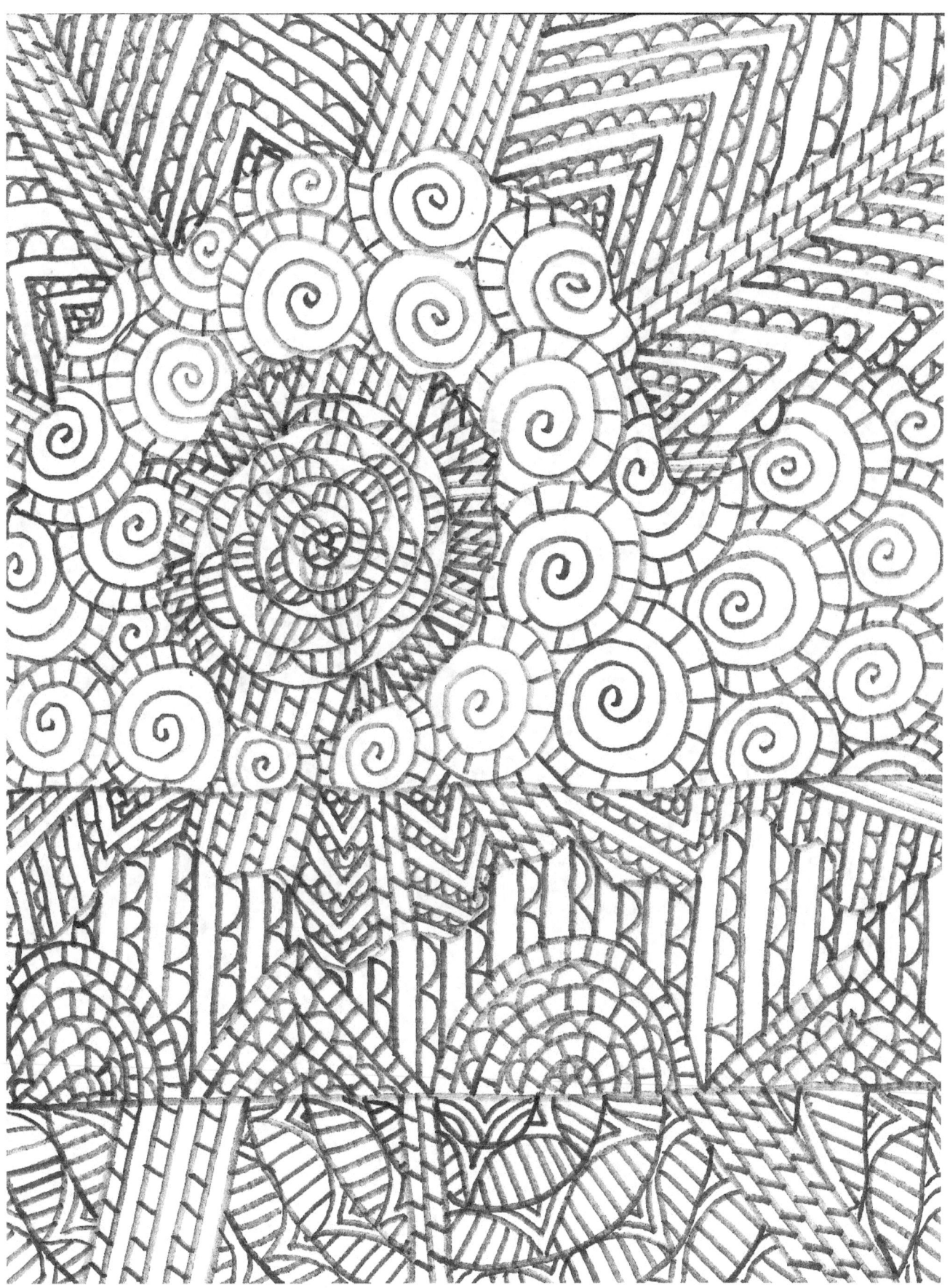

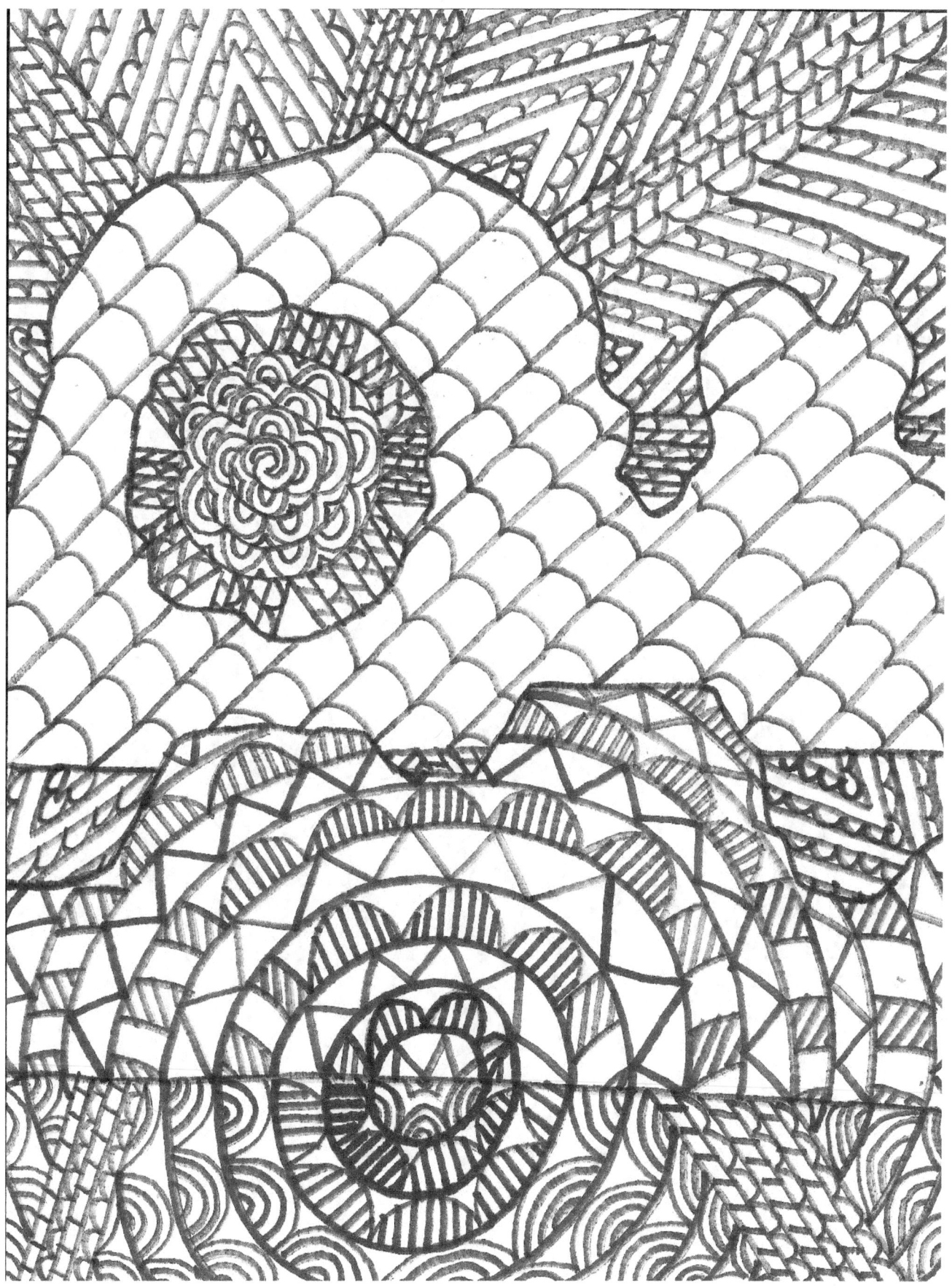

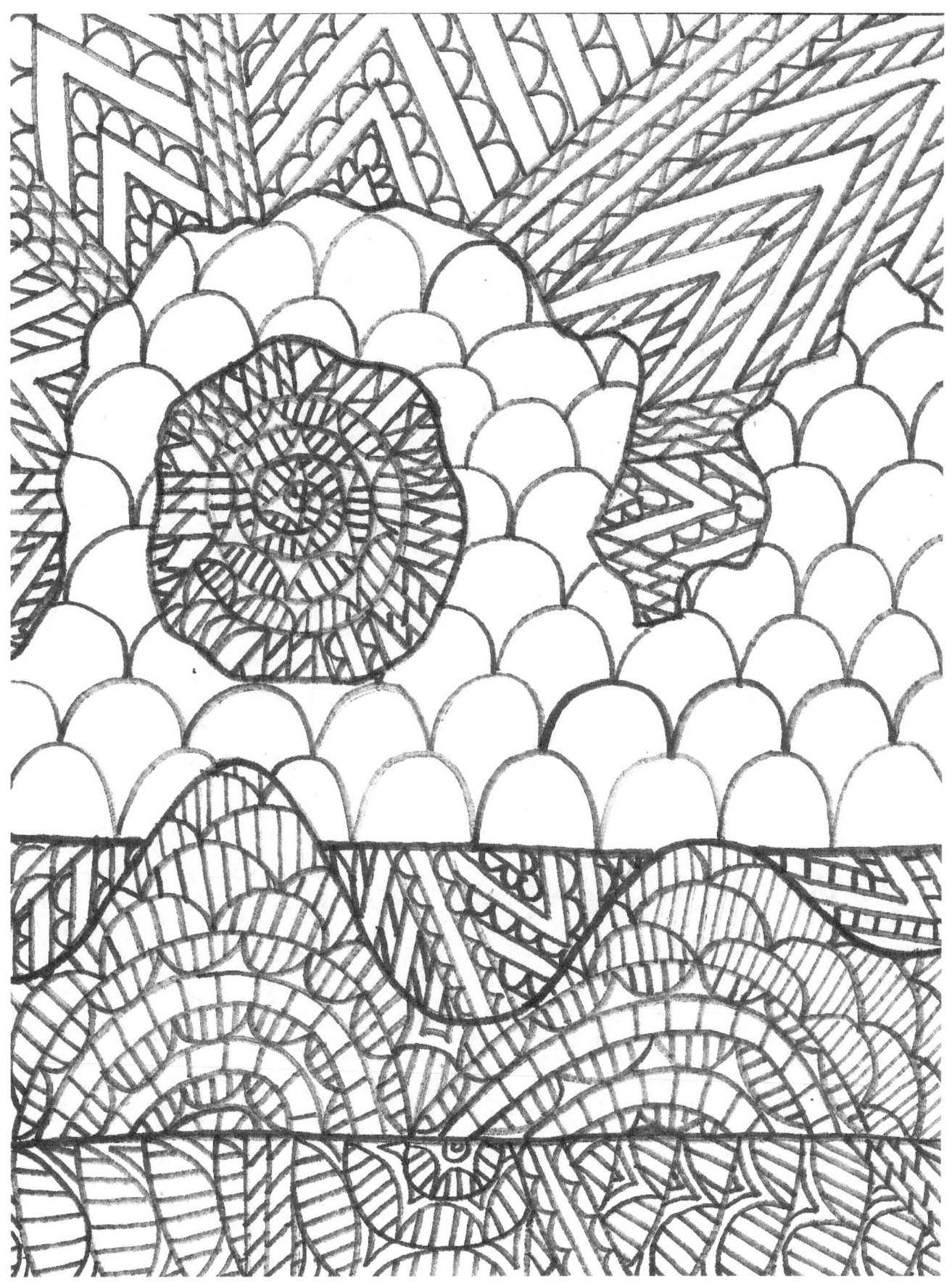

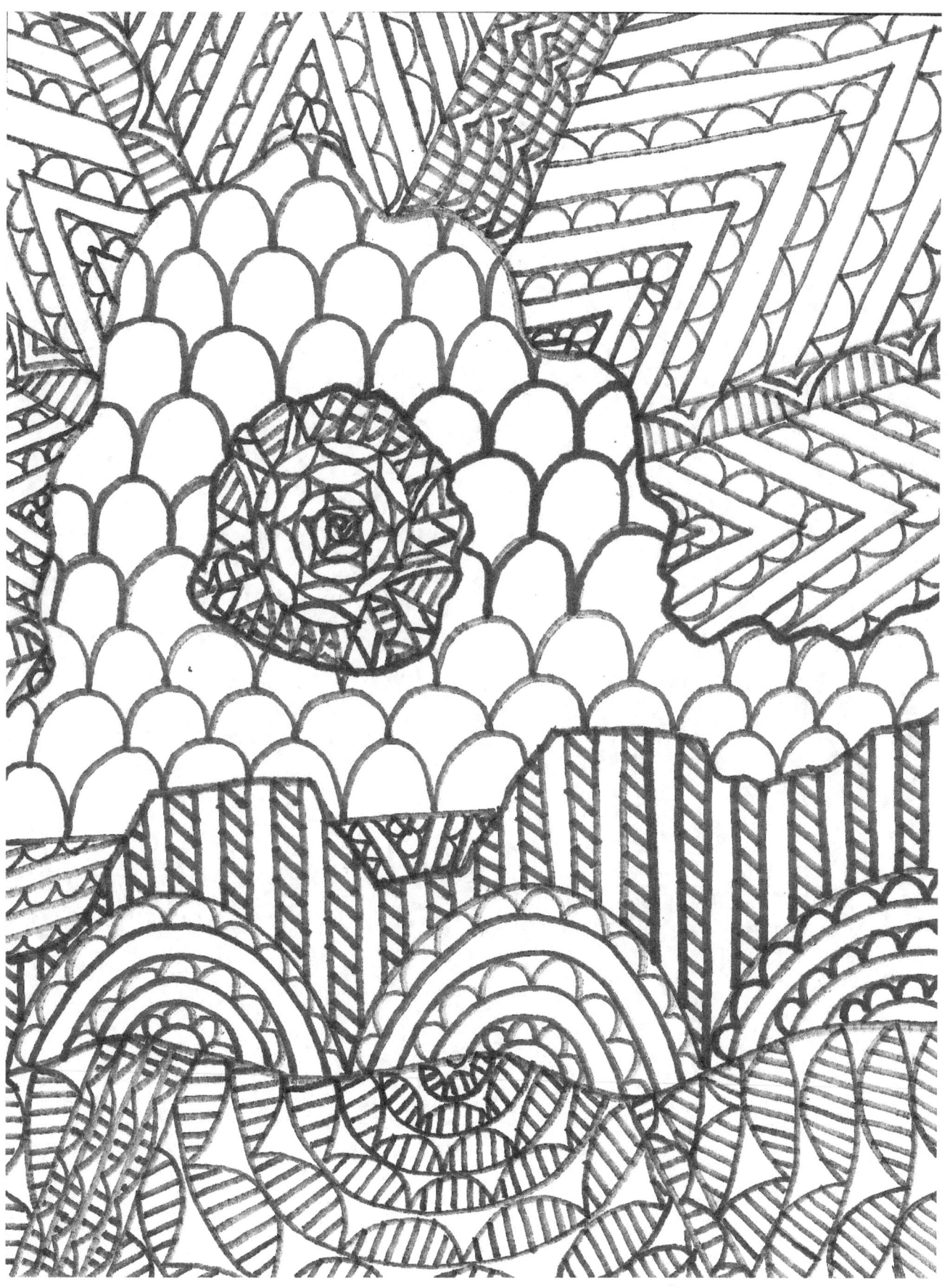

Bobby J. Jones

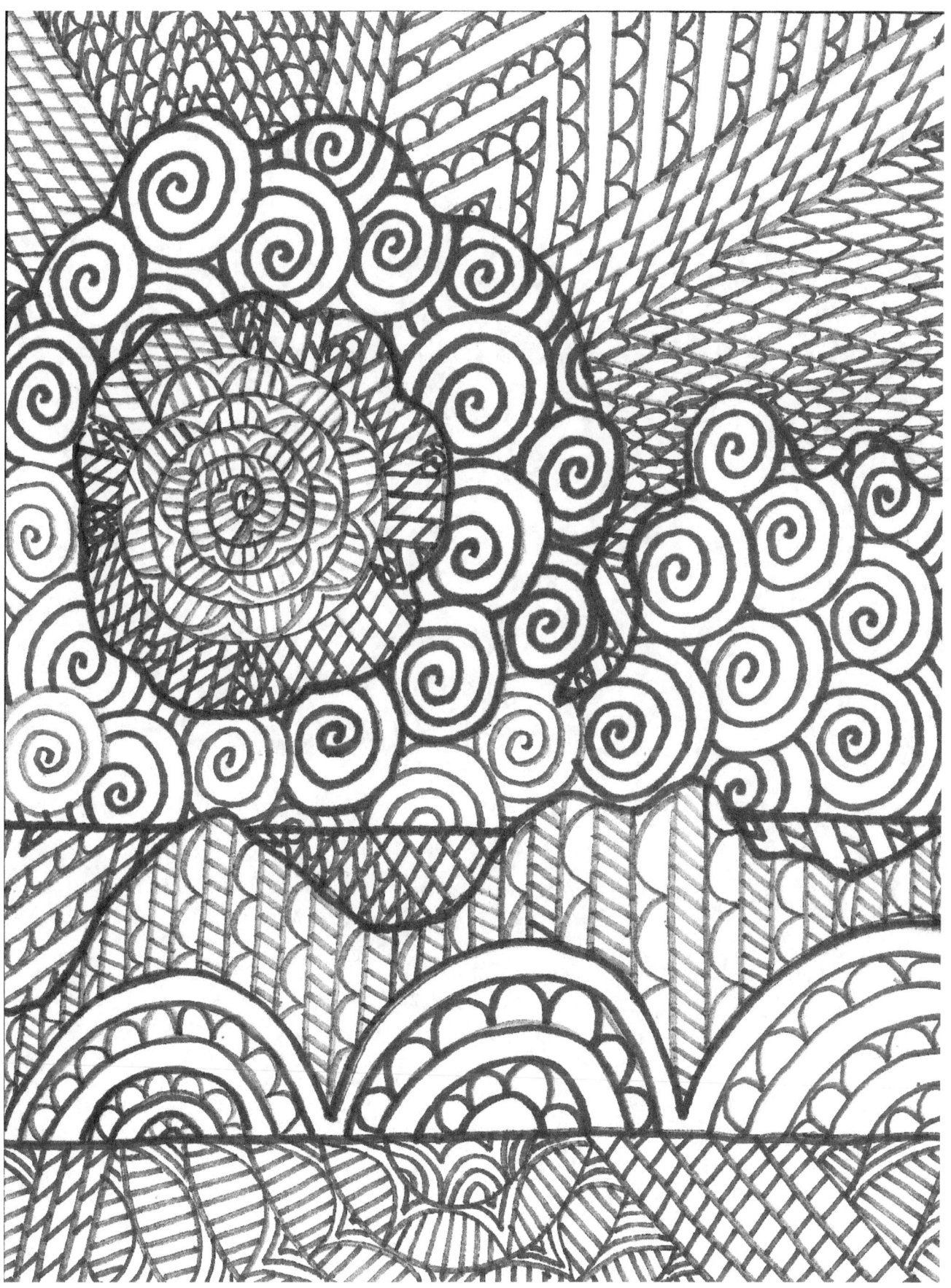

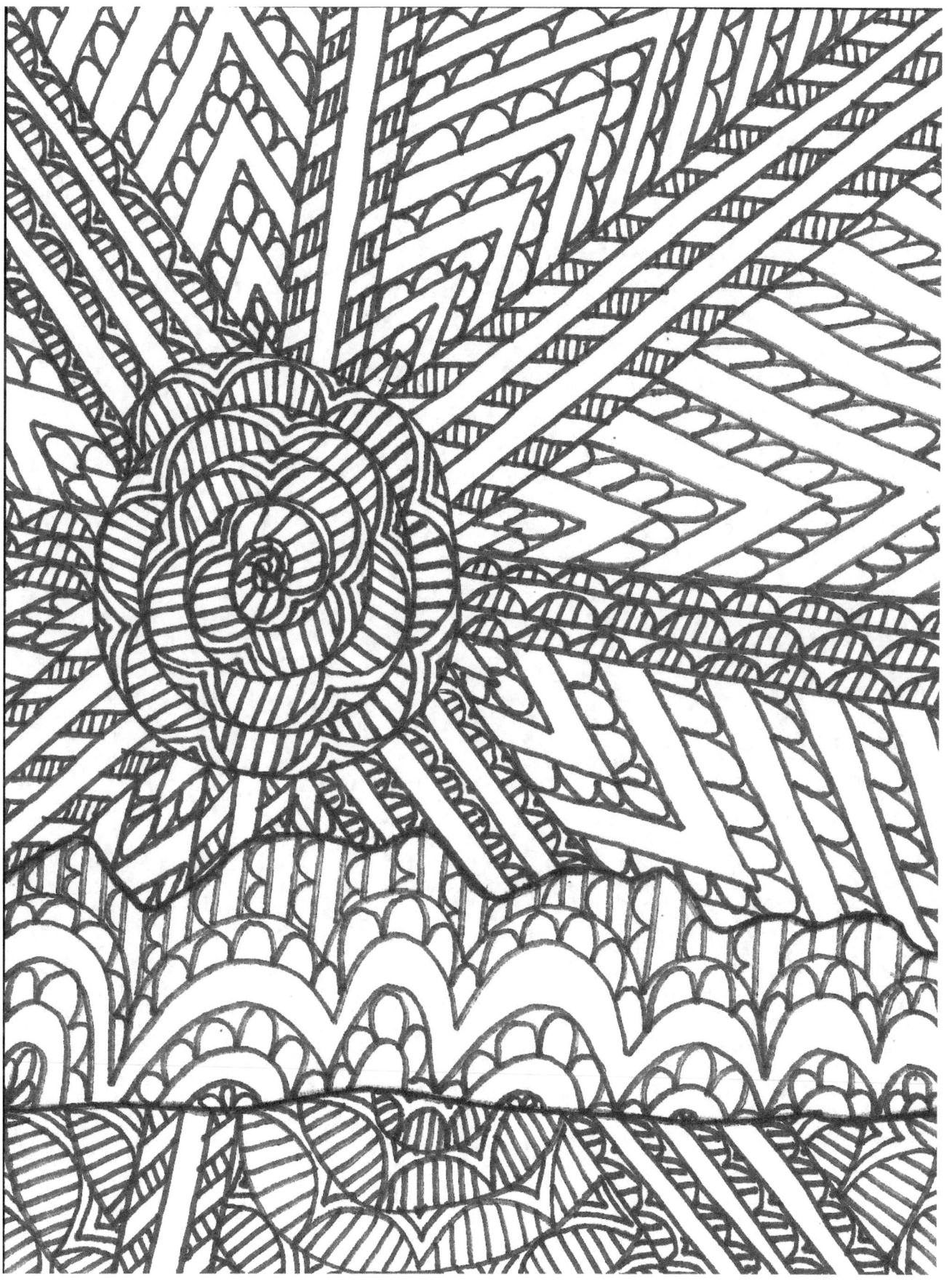

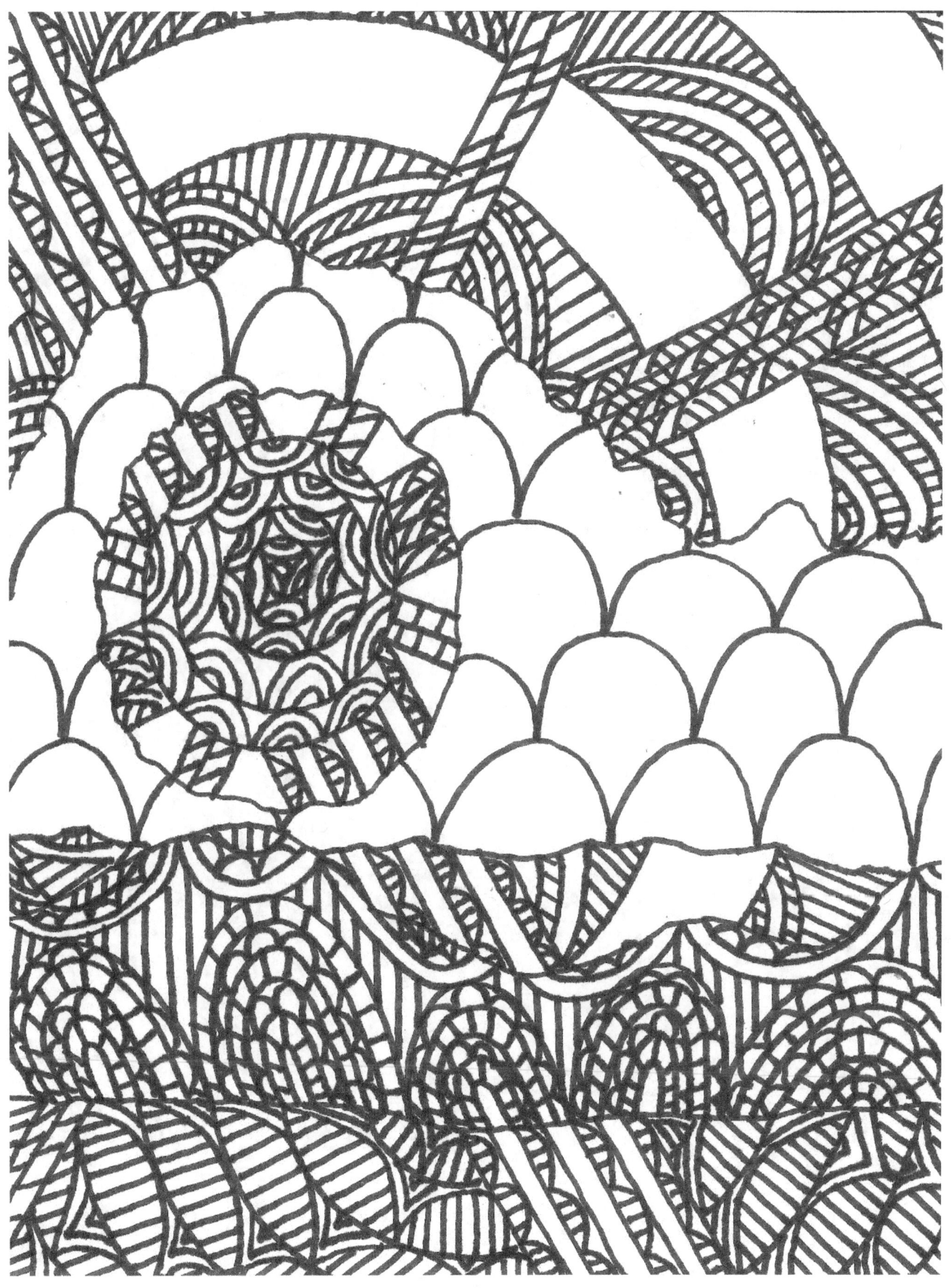

New Mexico Dreamscapes II

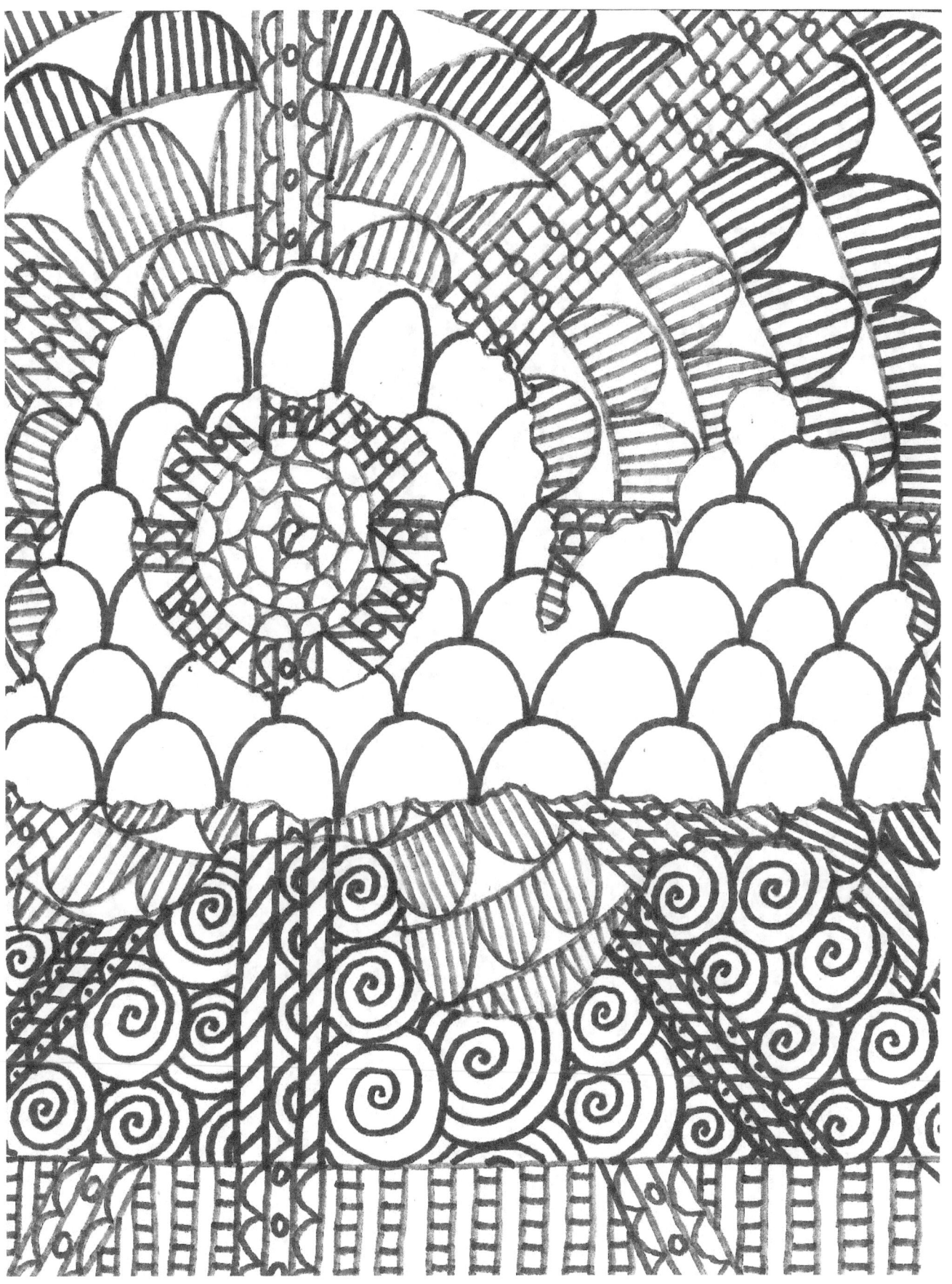

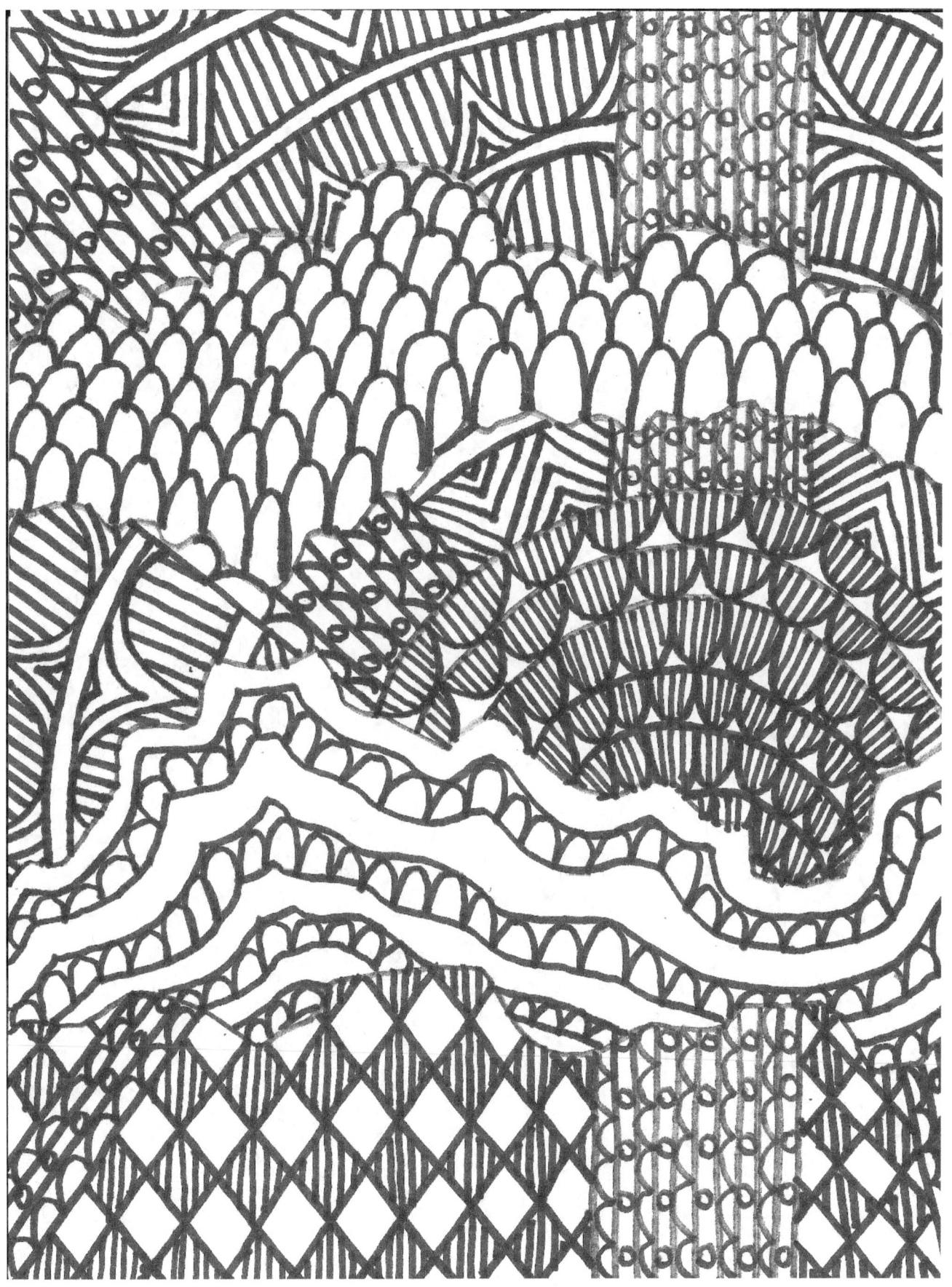

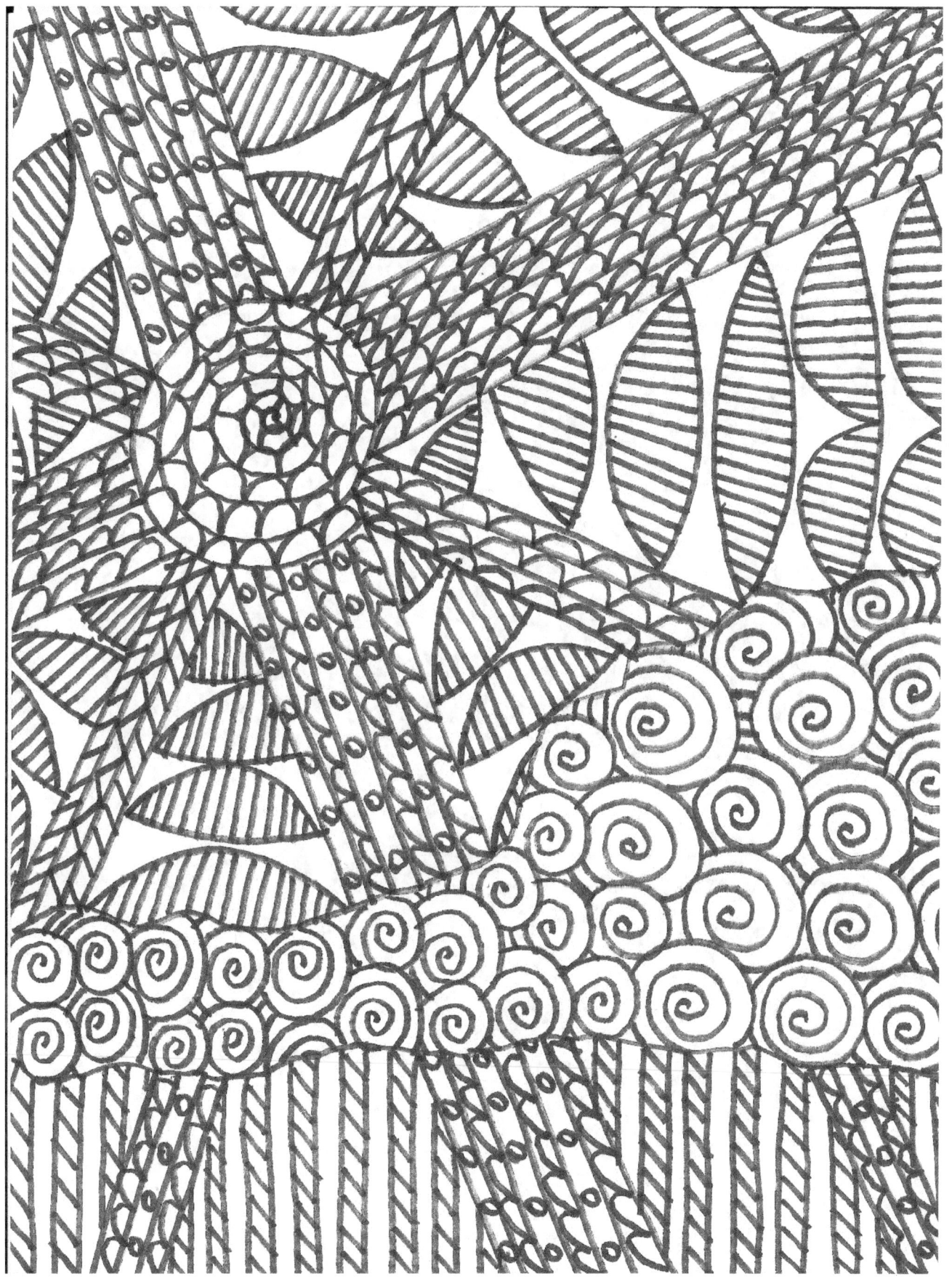

Bobby J. Jones

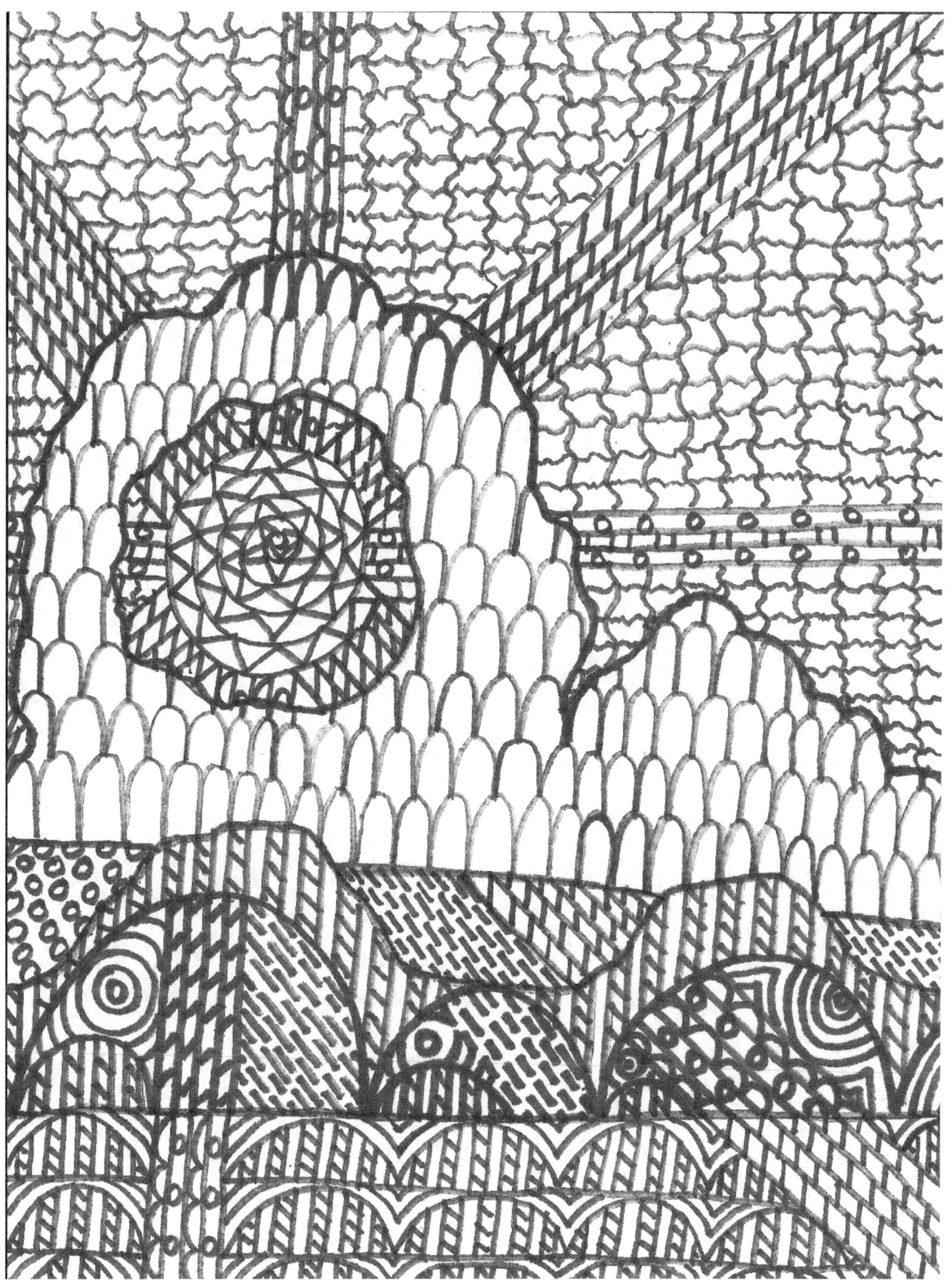

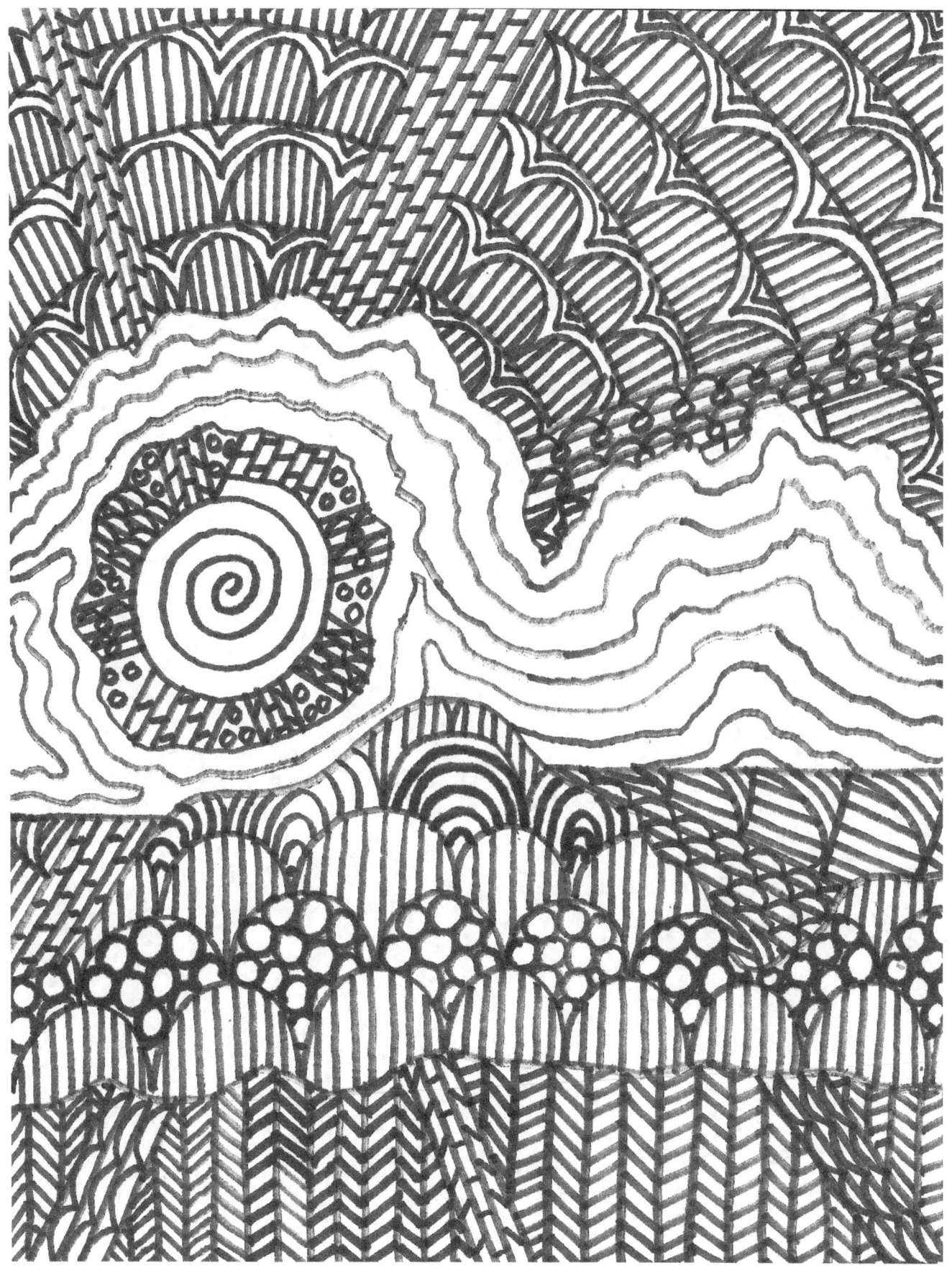

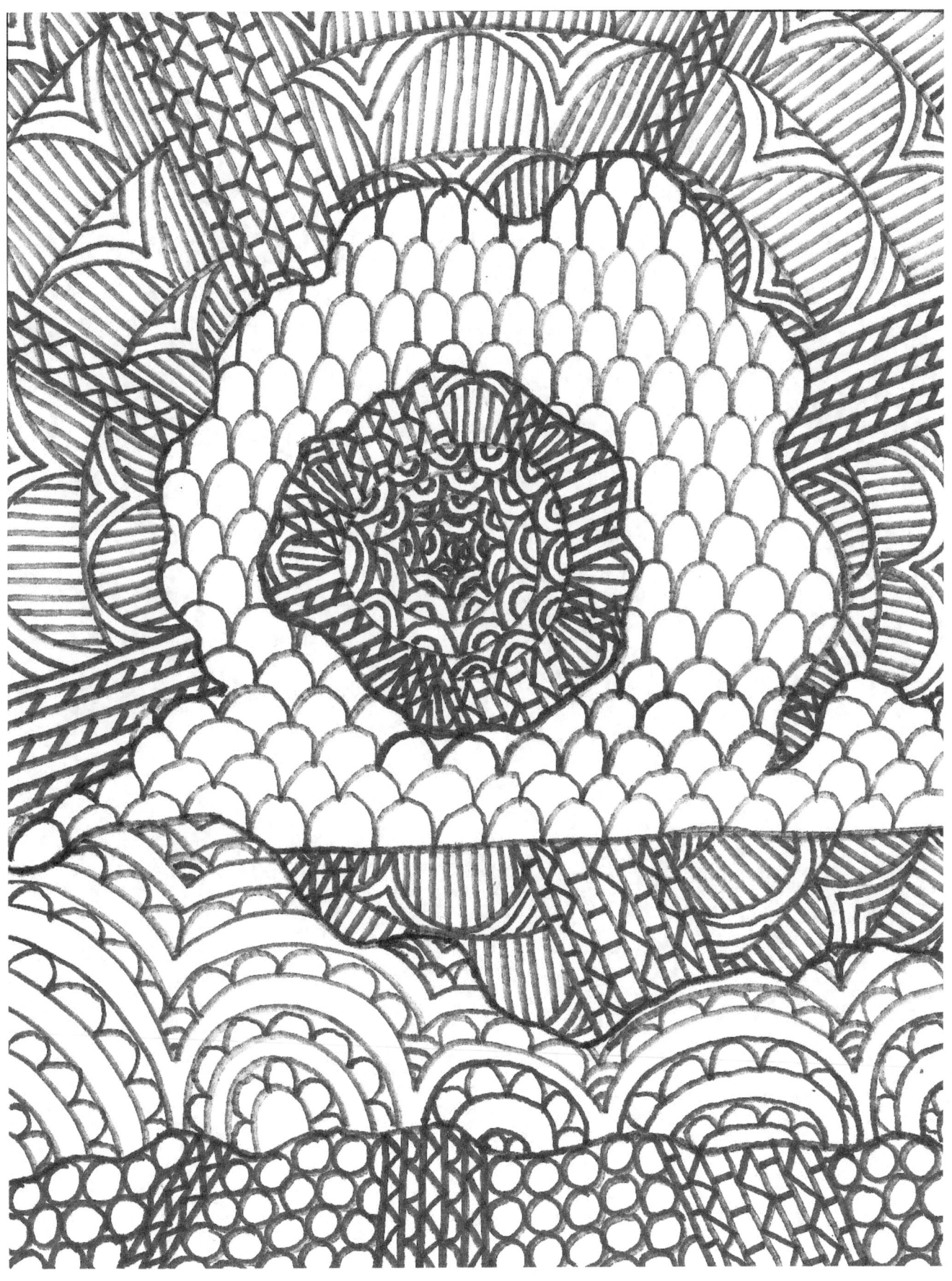

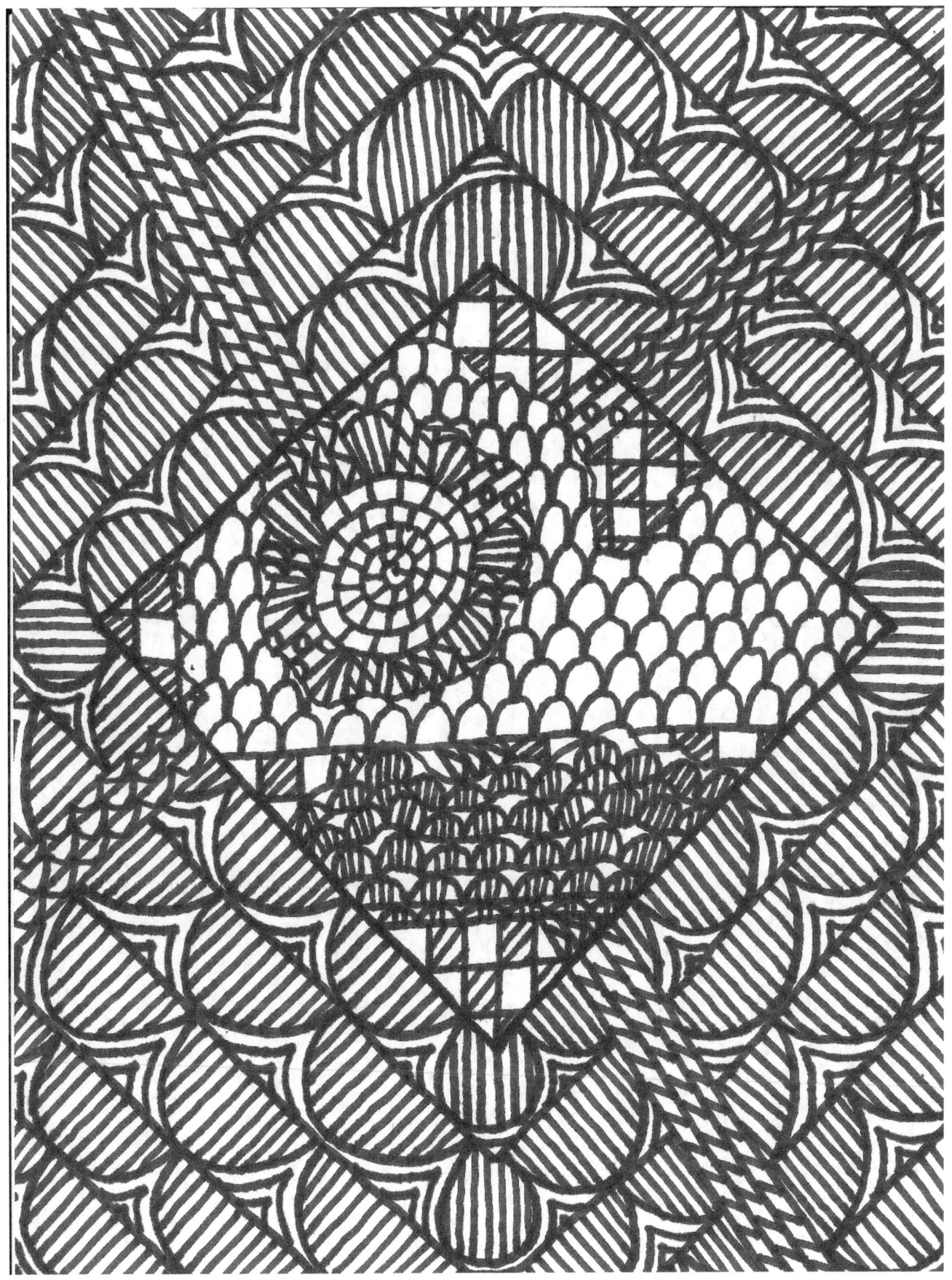

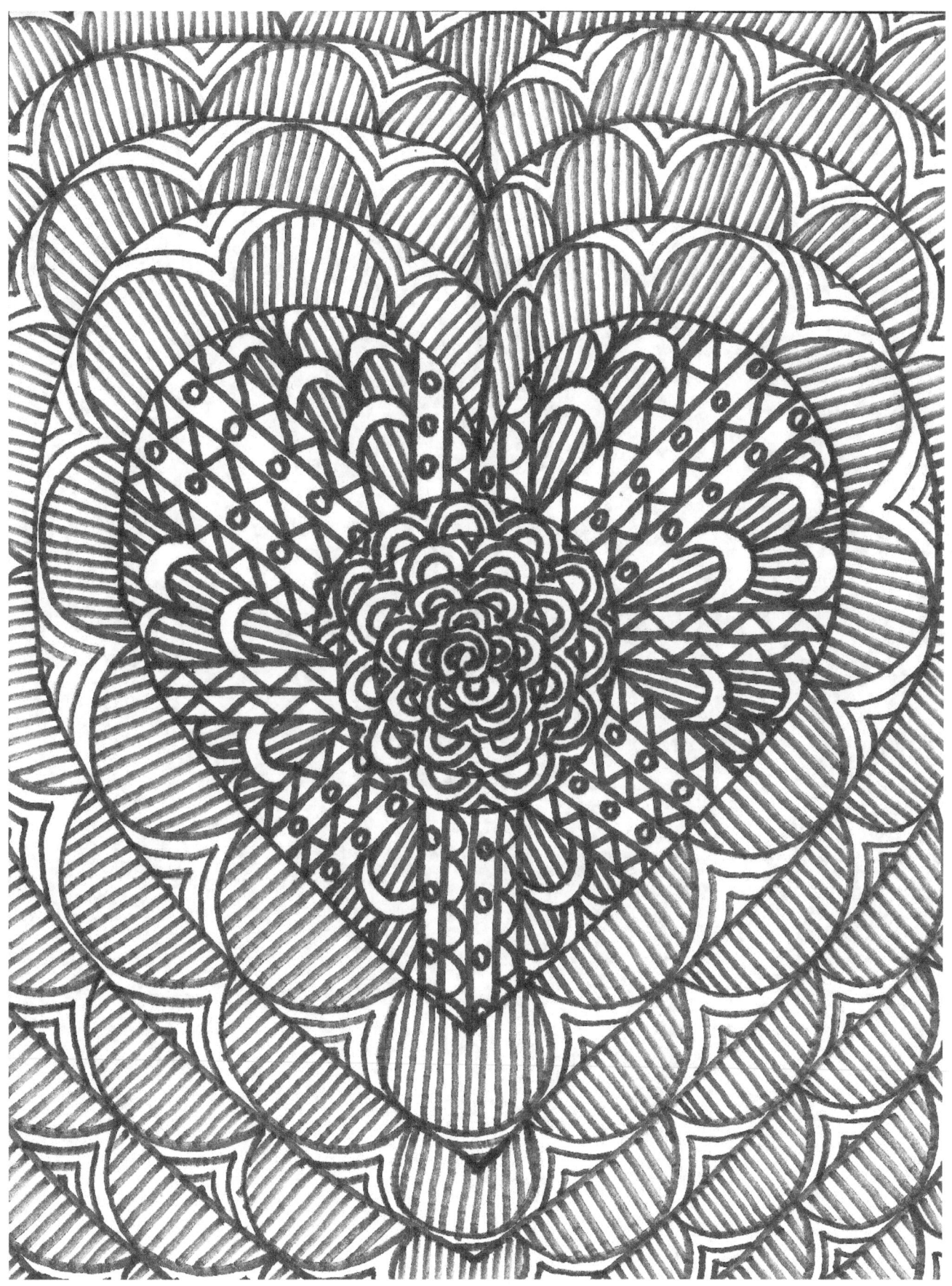

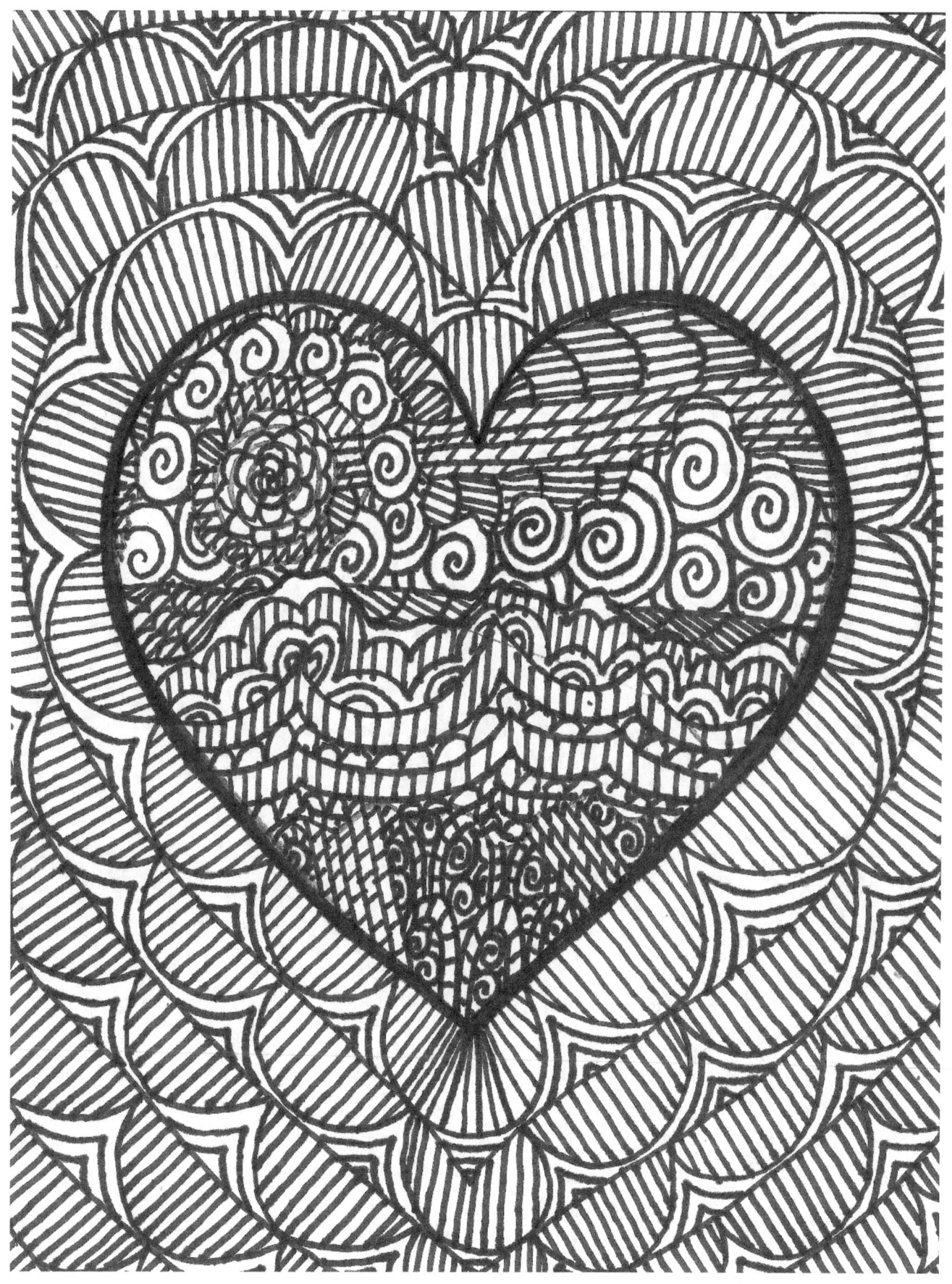

Bobby J. Jones

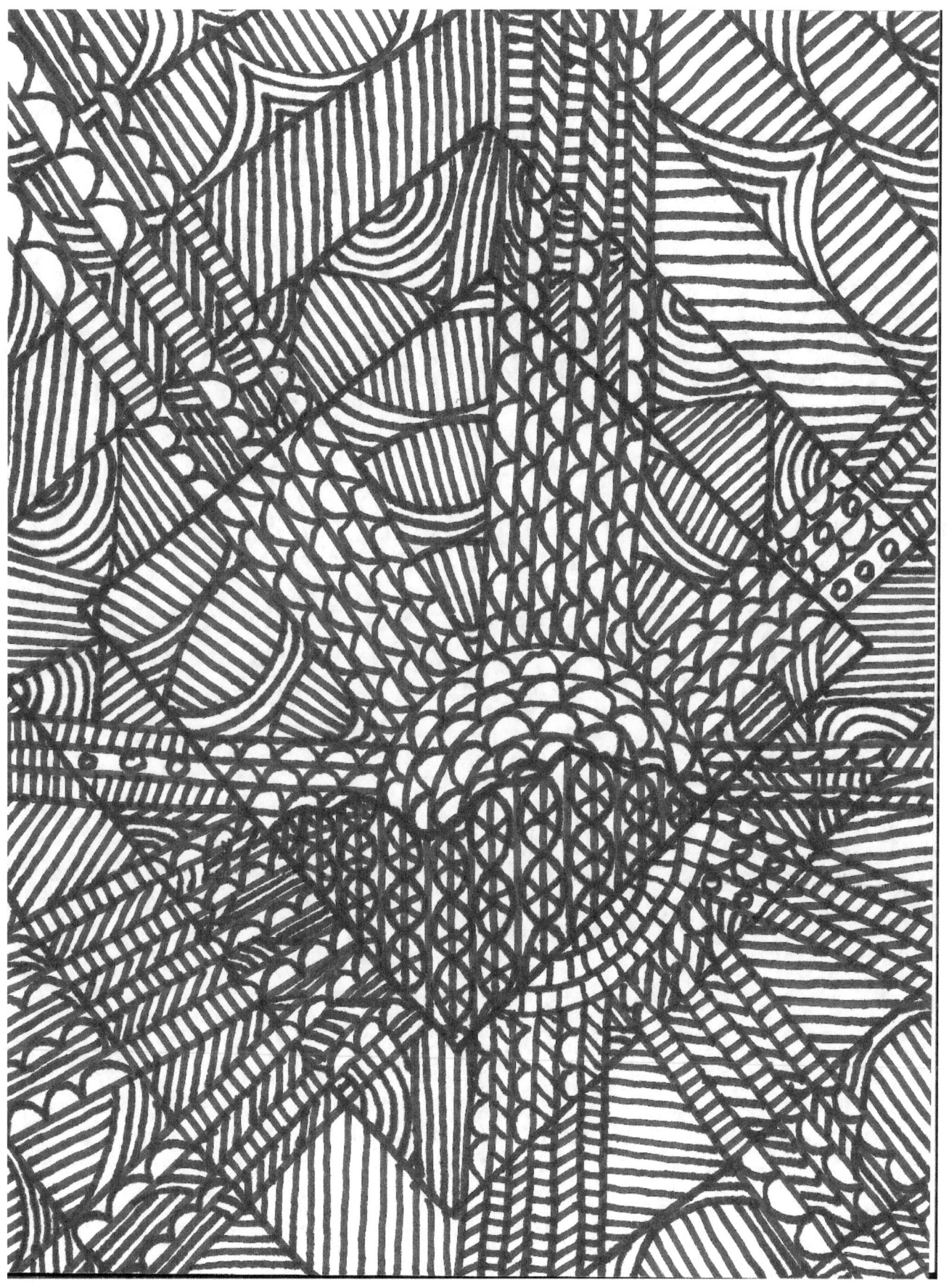

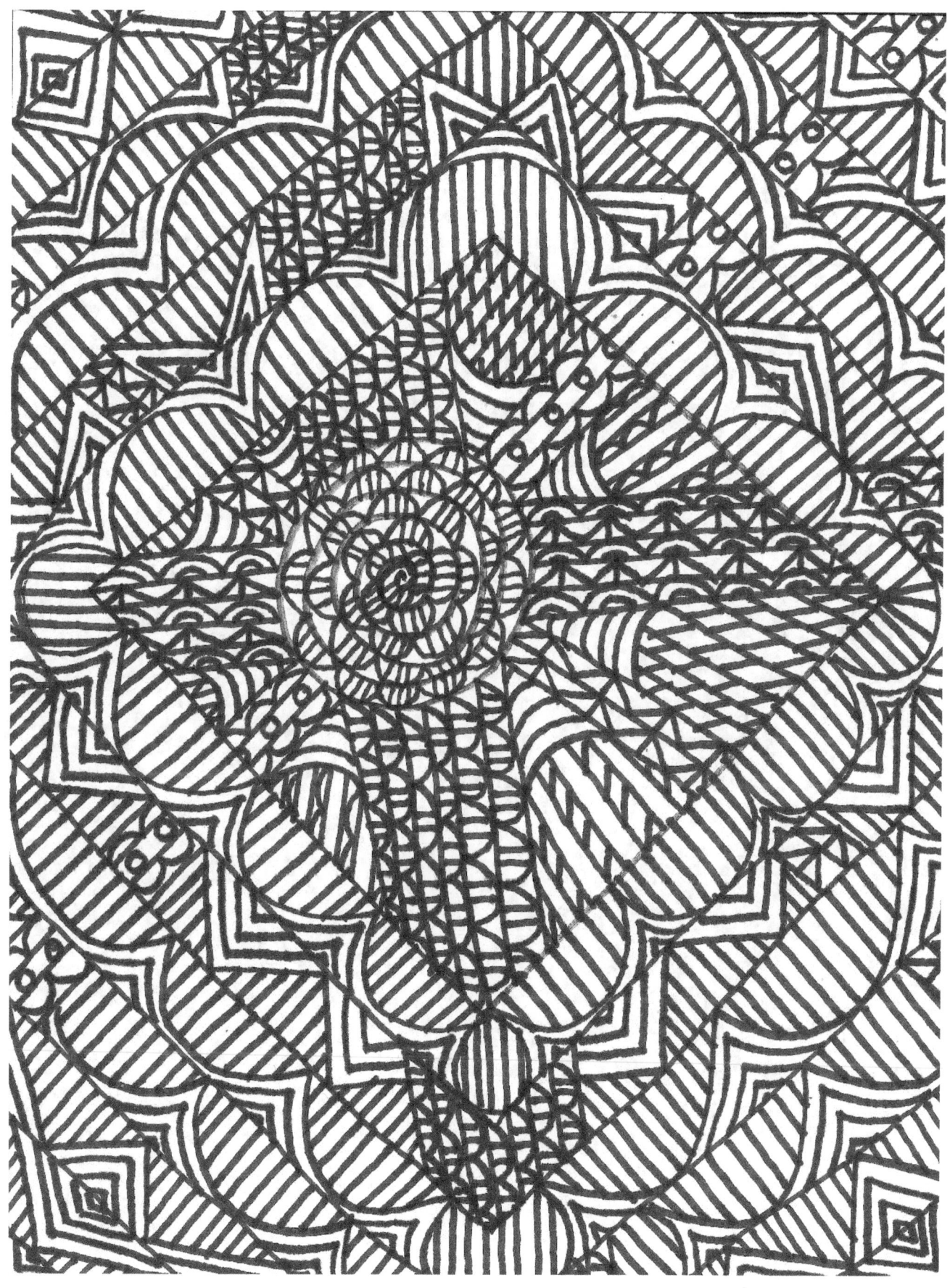

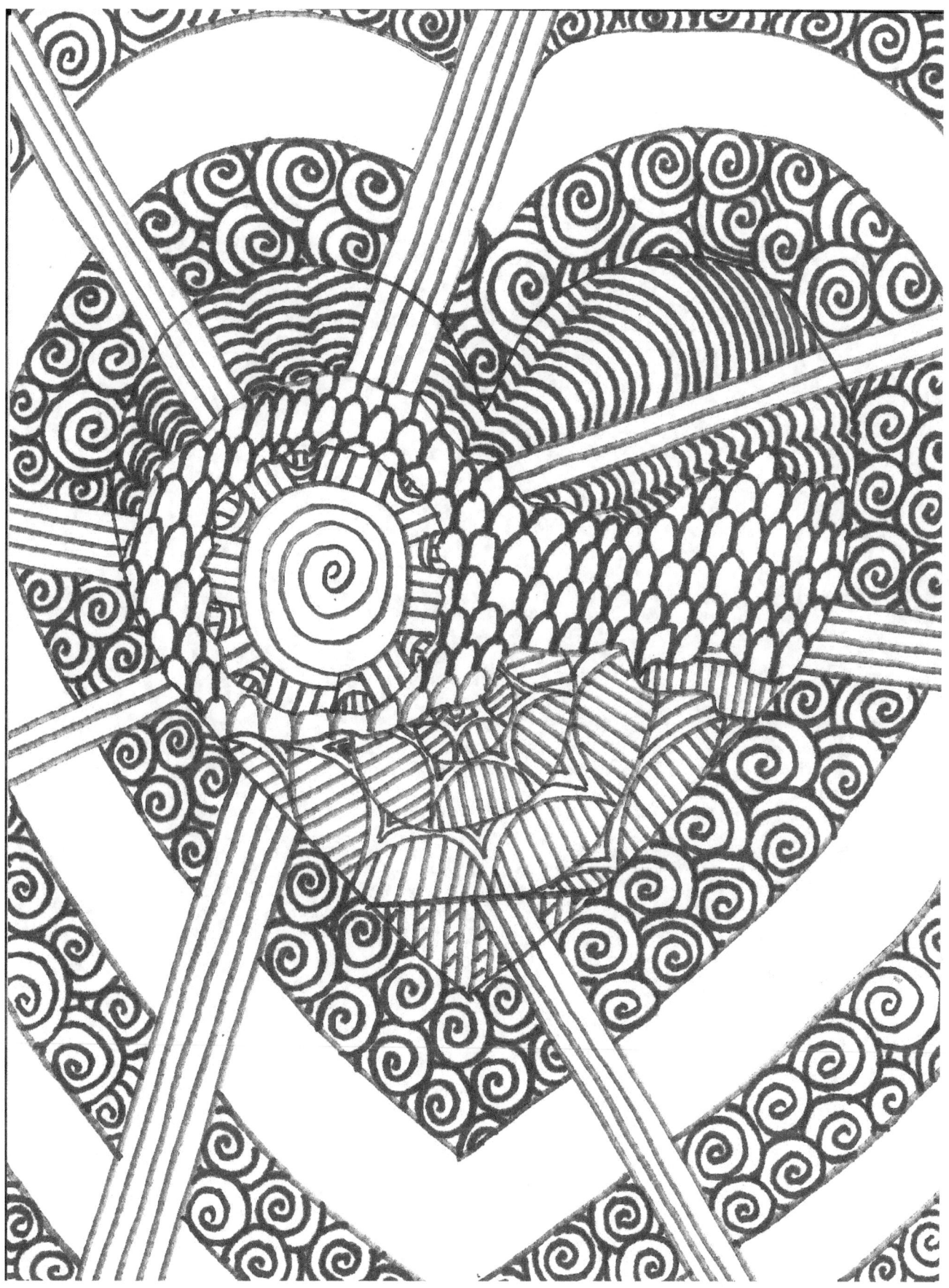

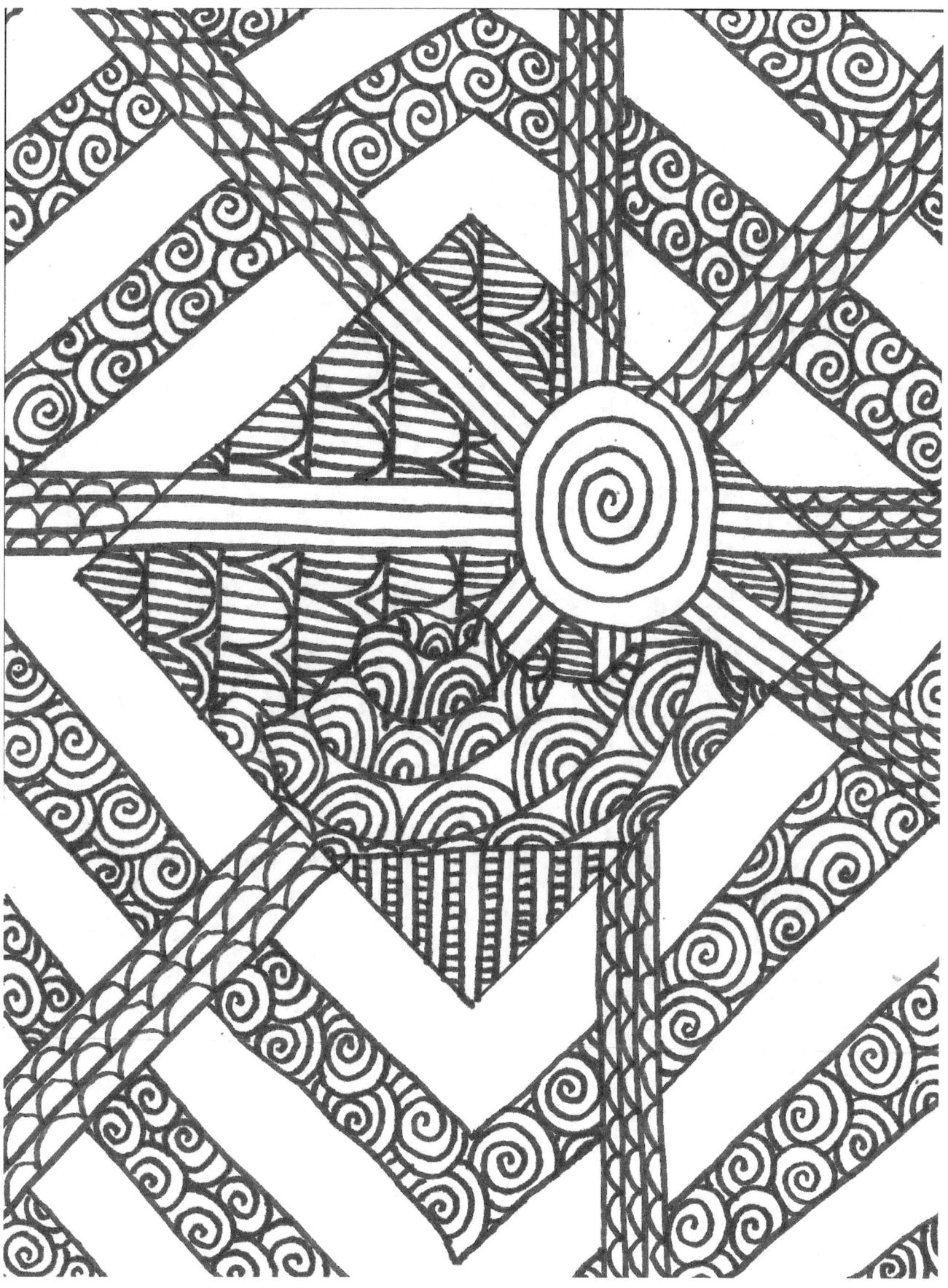

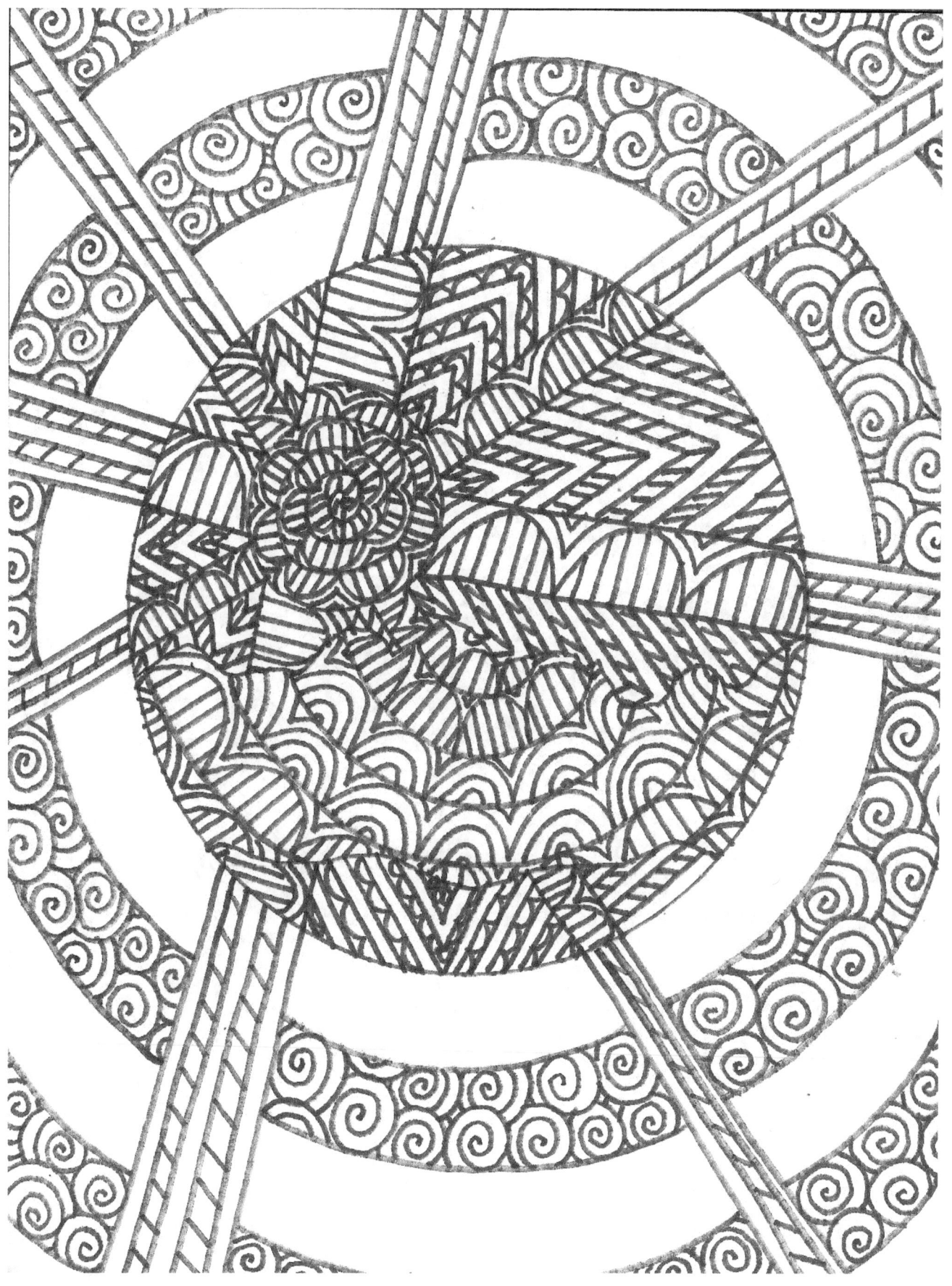

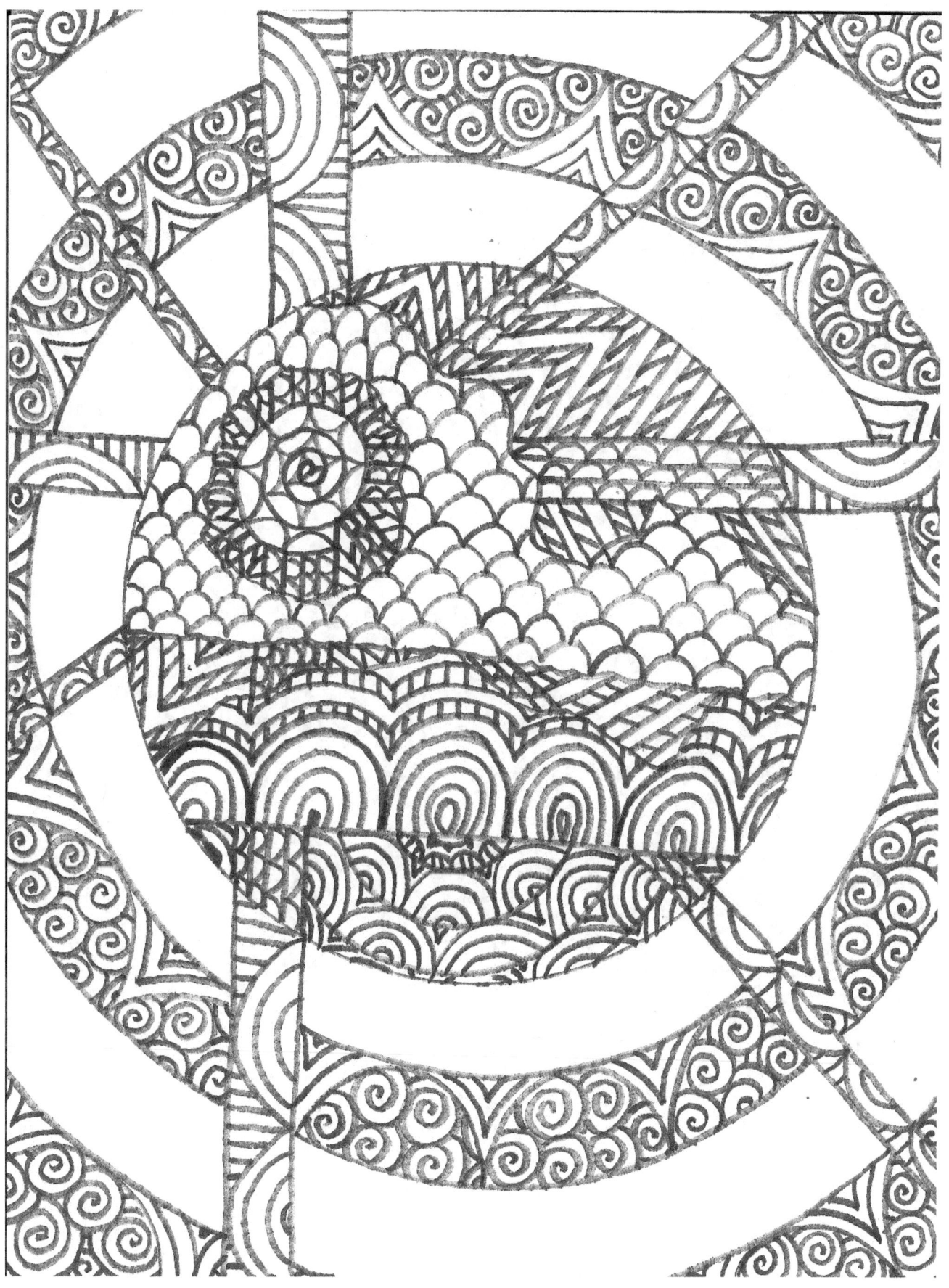

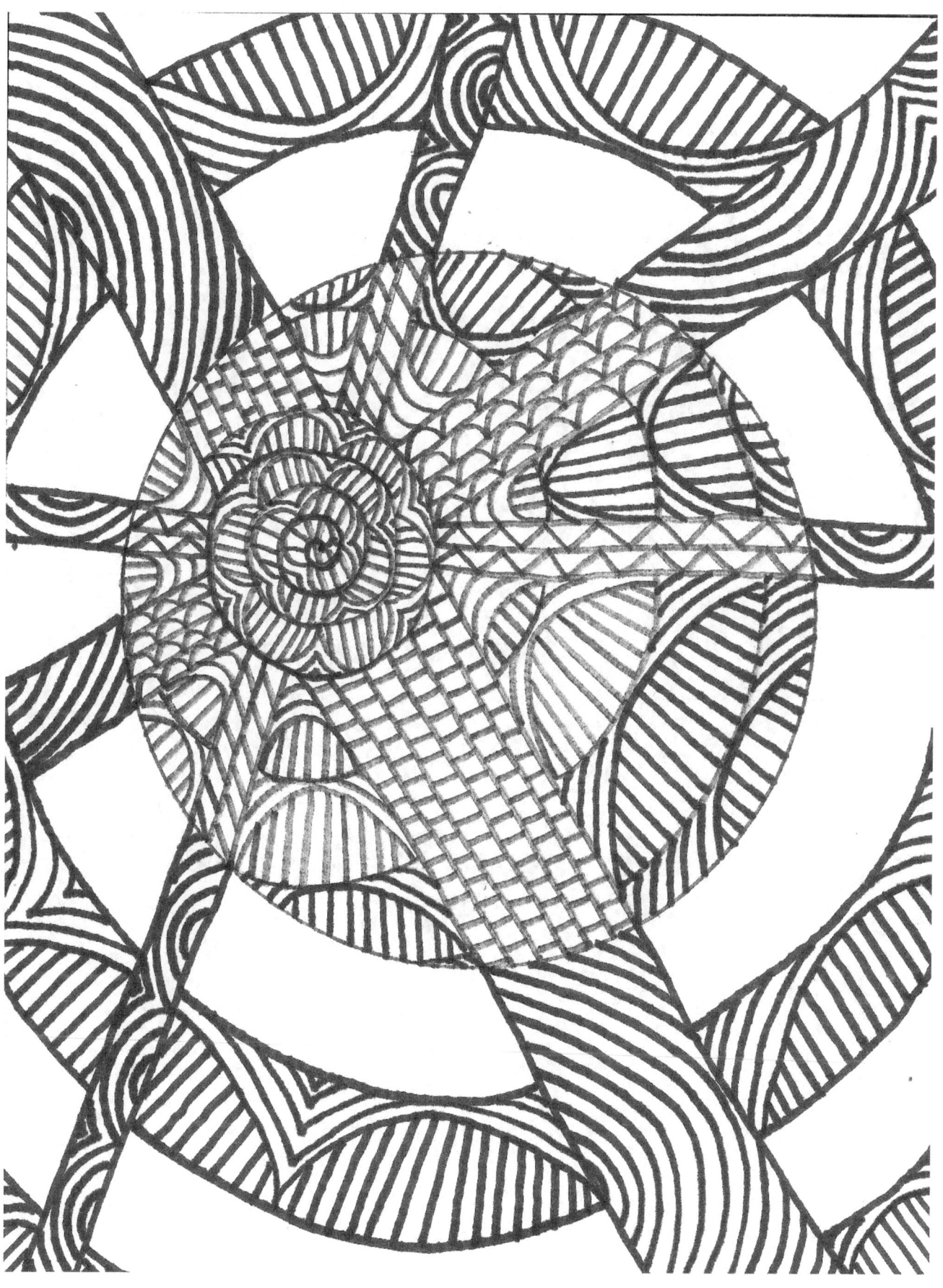

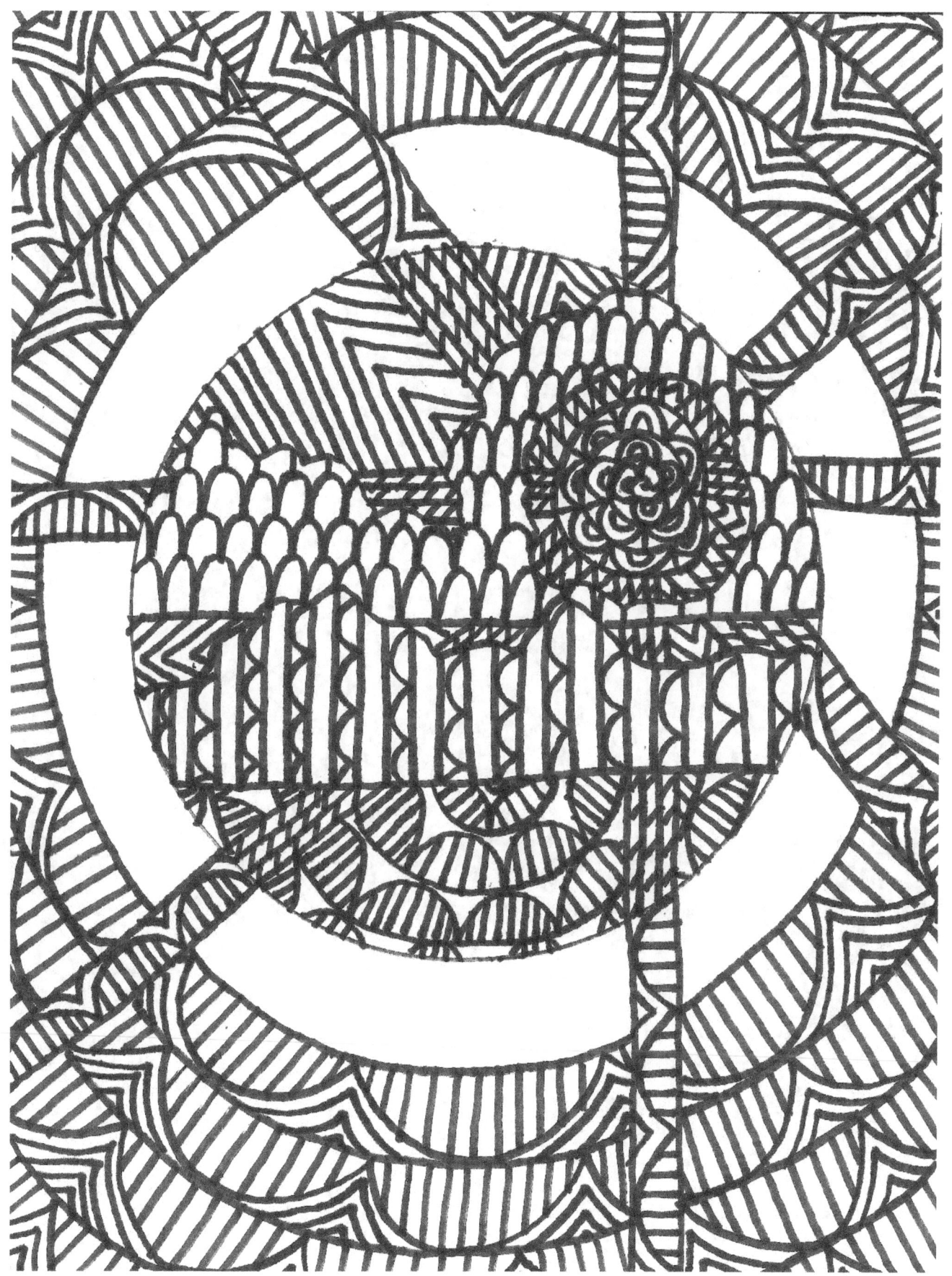

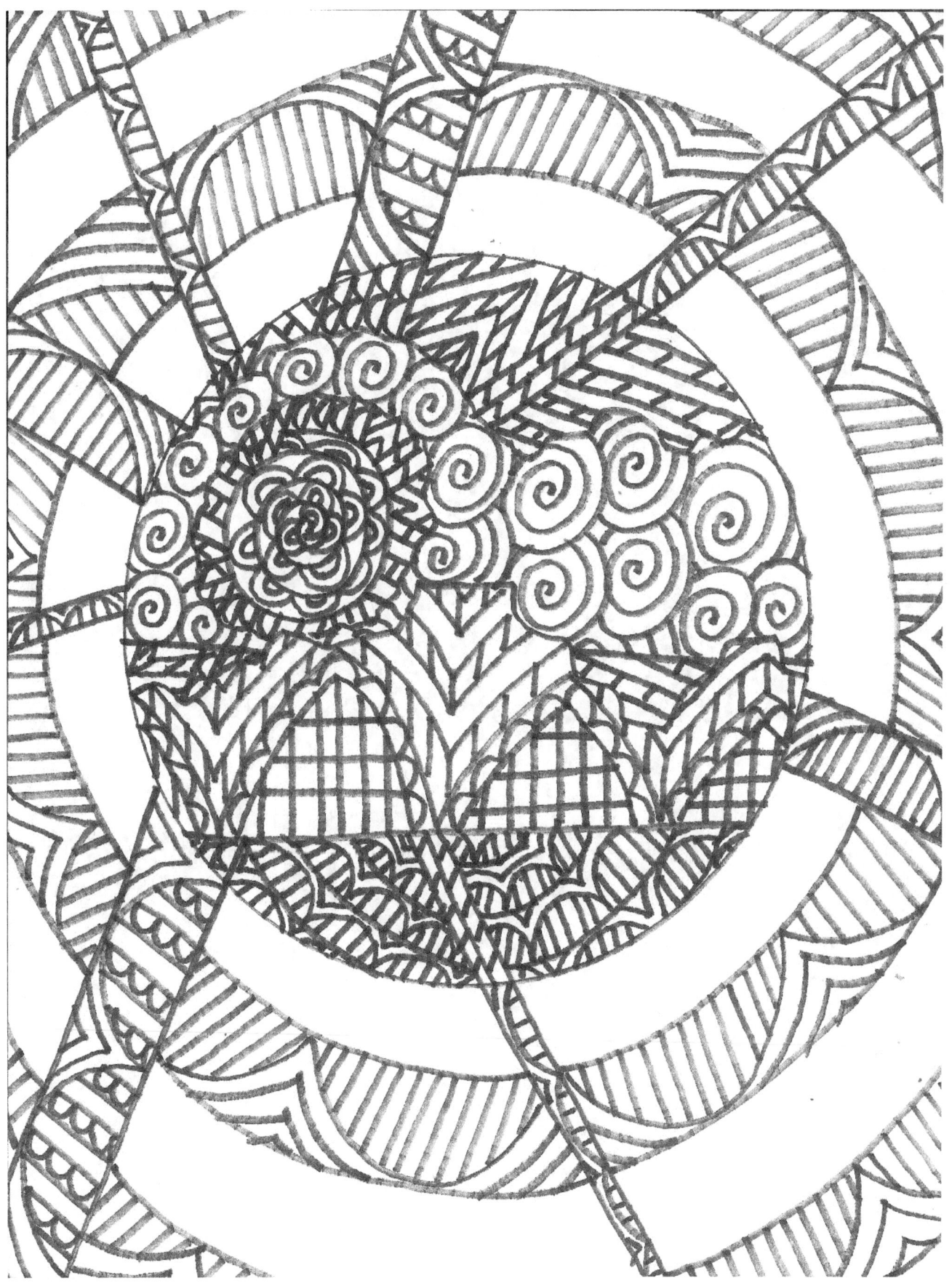

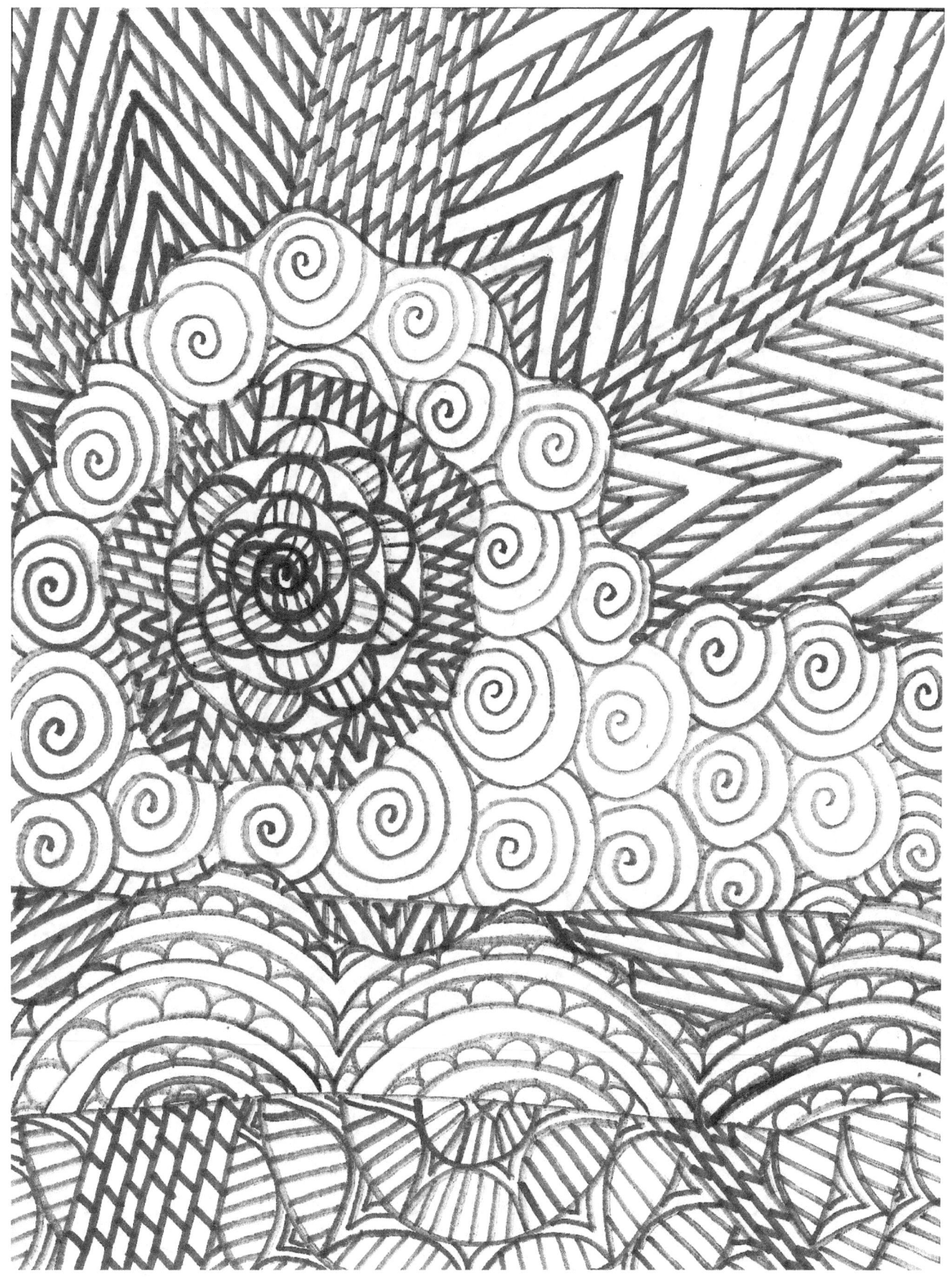

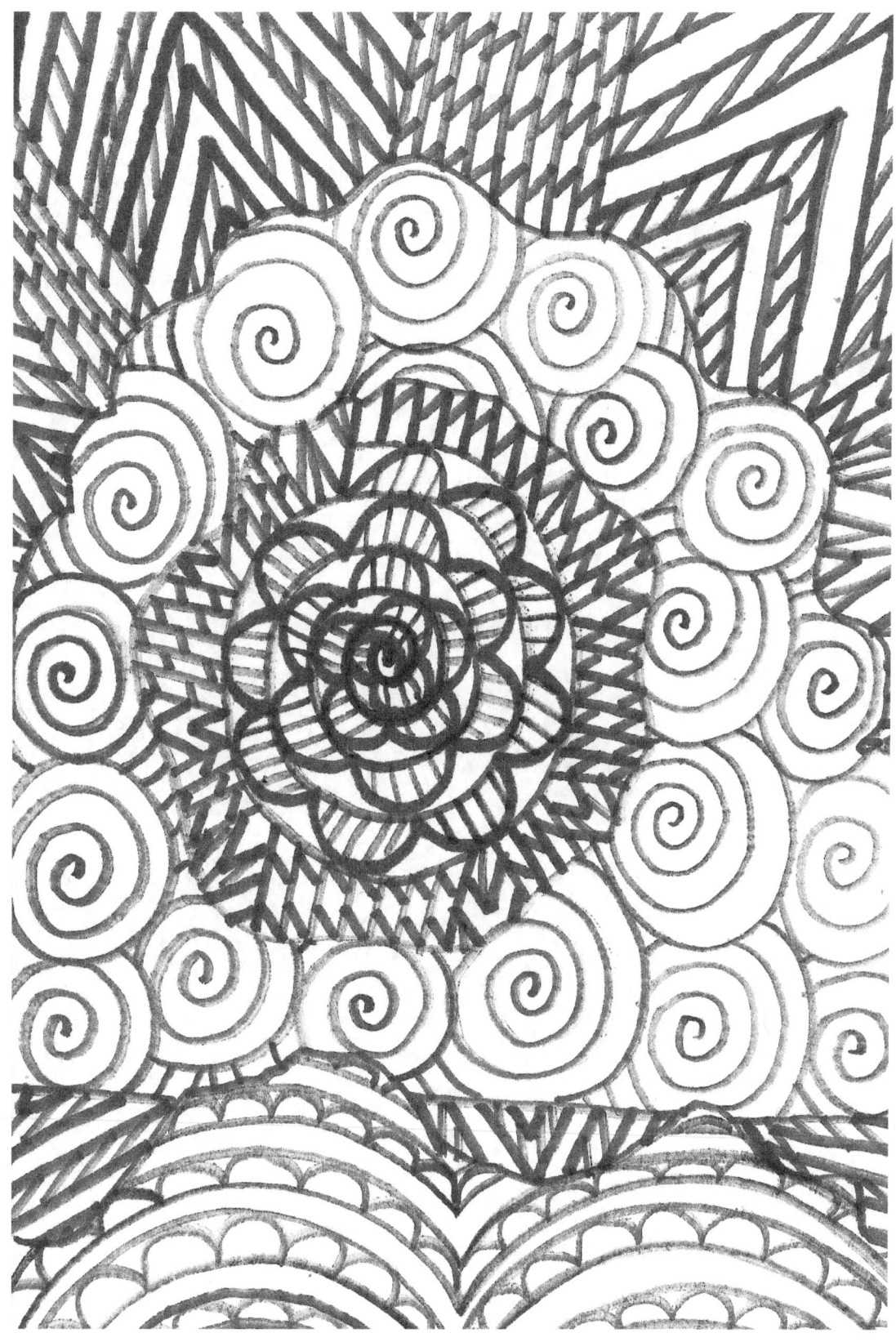

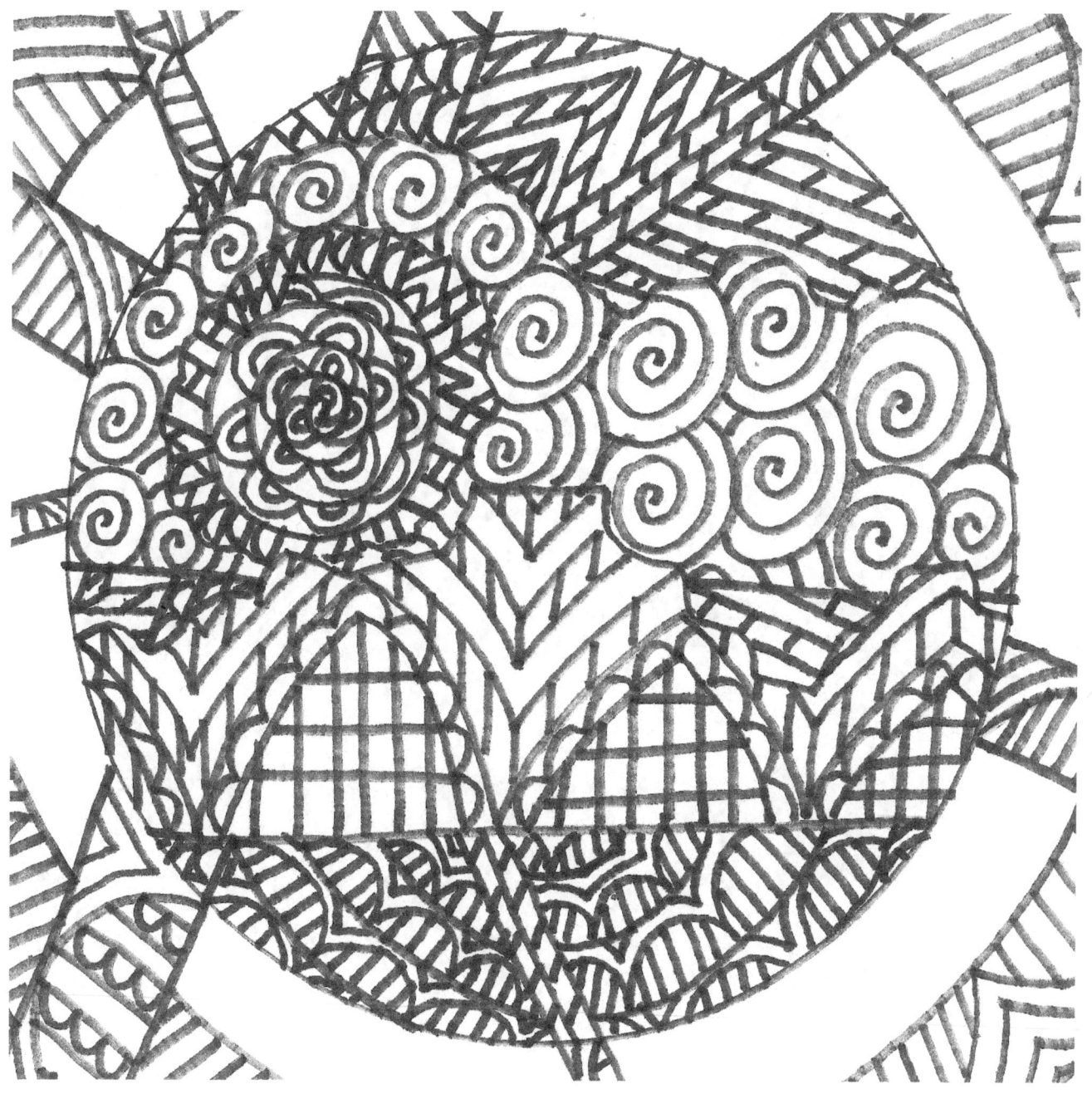

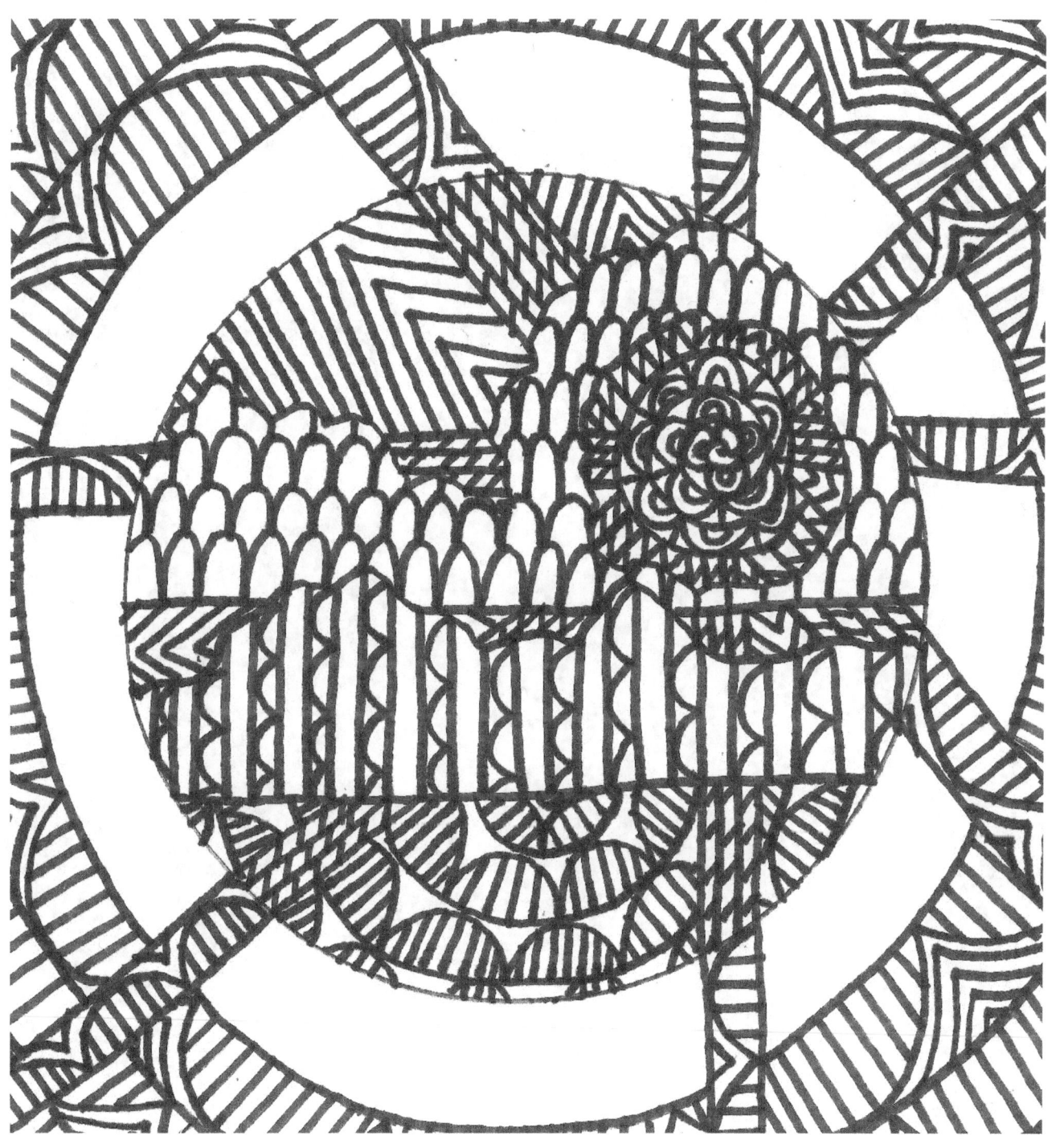

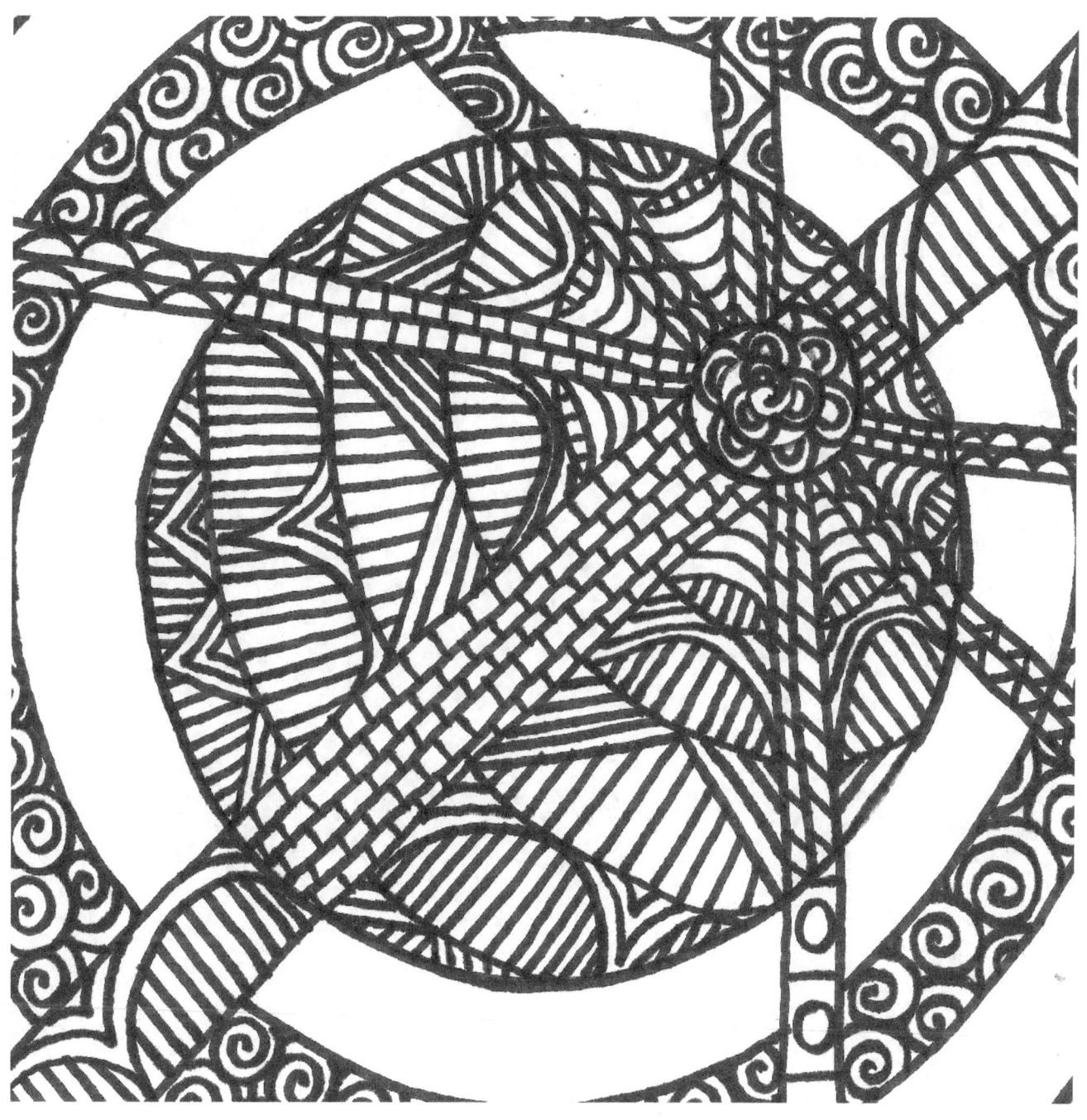

Bobby J. Jones

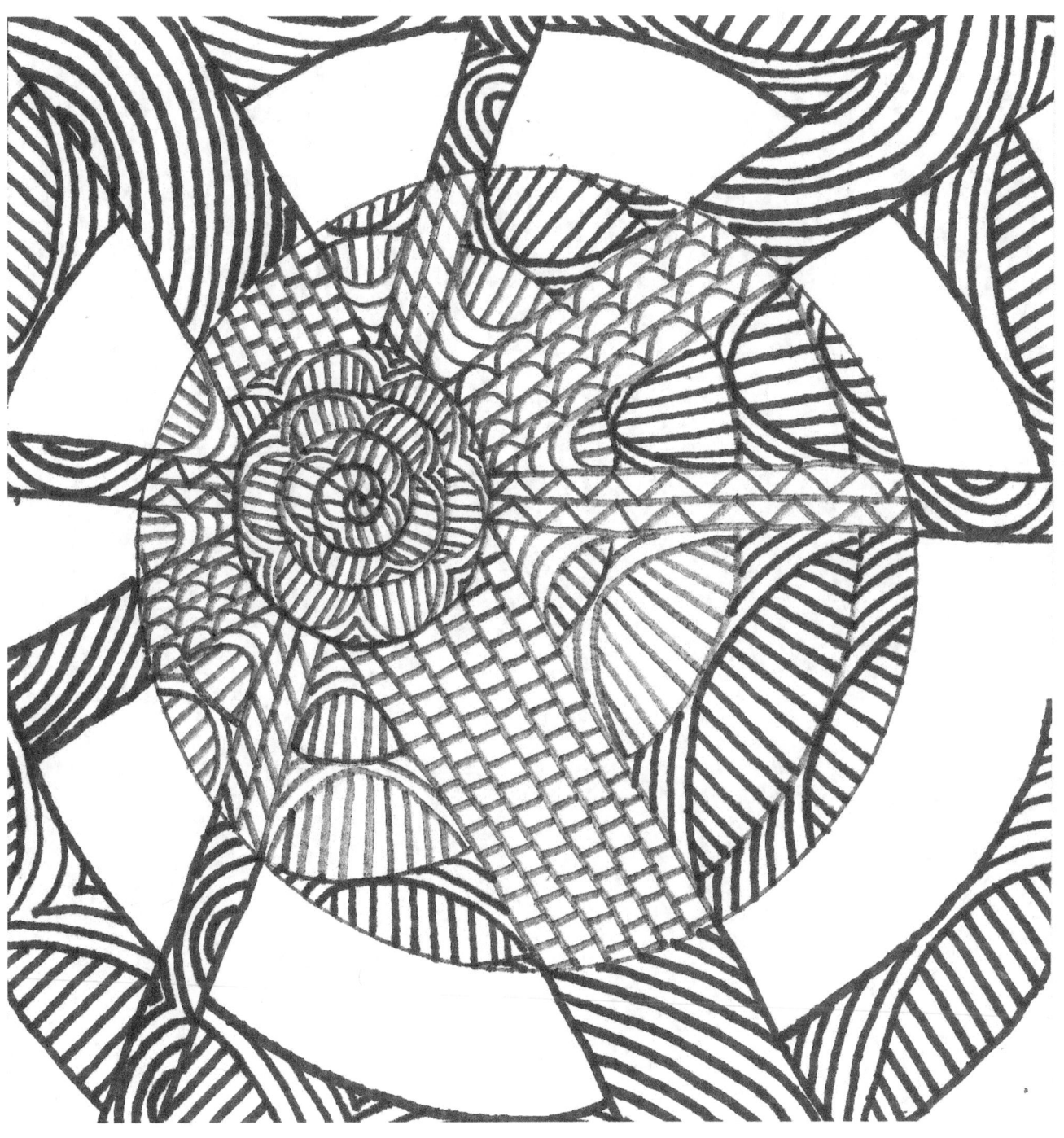

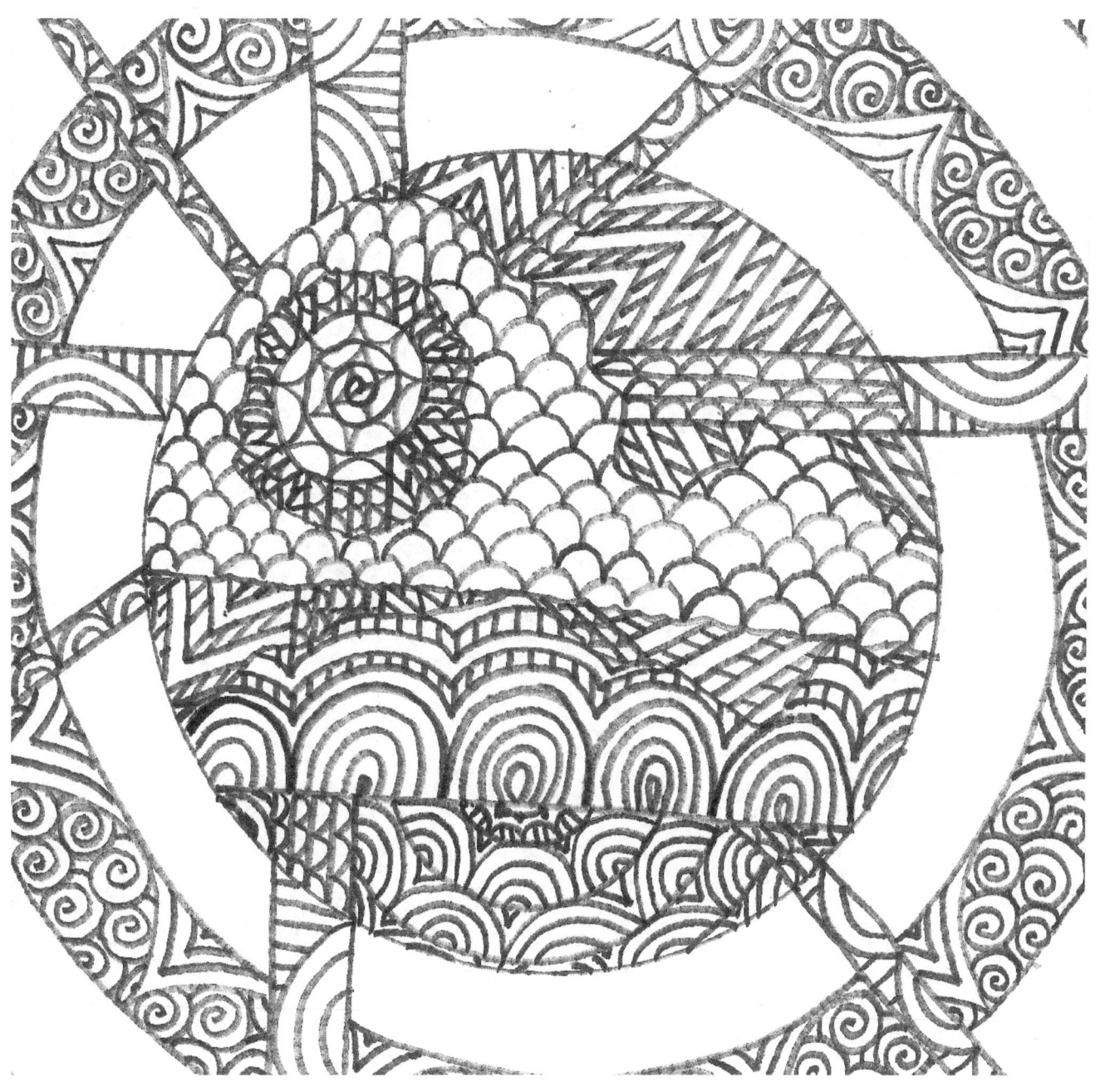

New Mexico Dreamscapes II

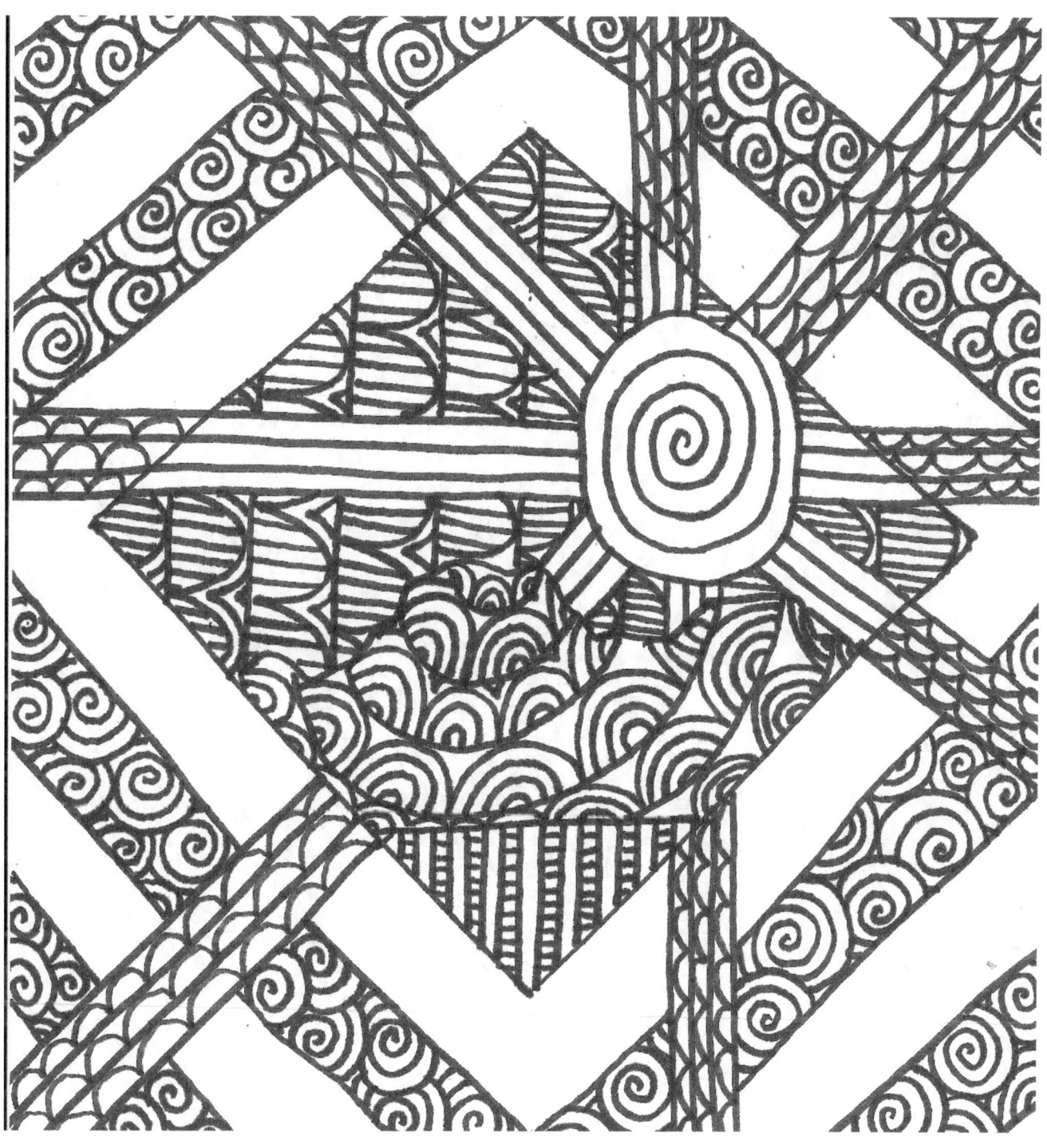

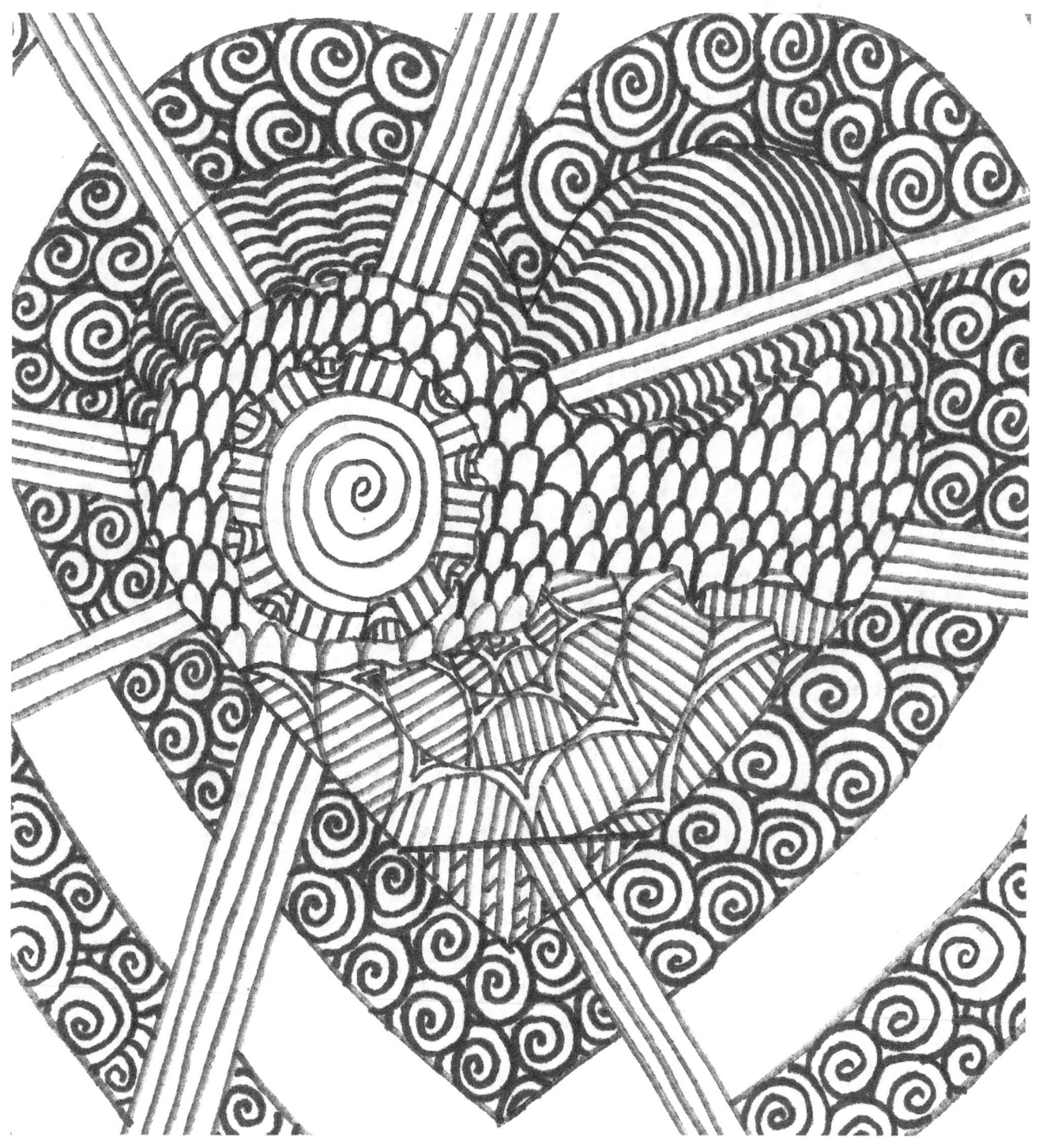

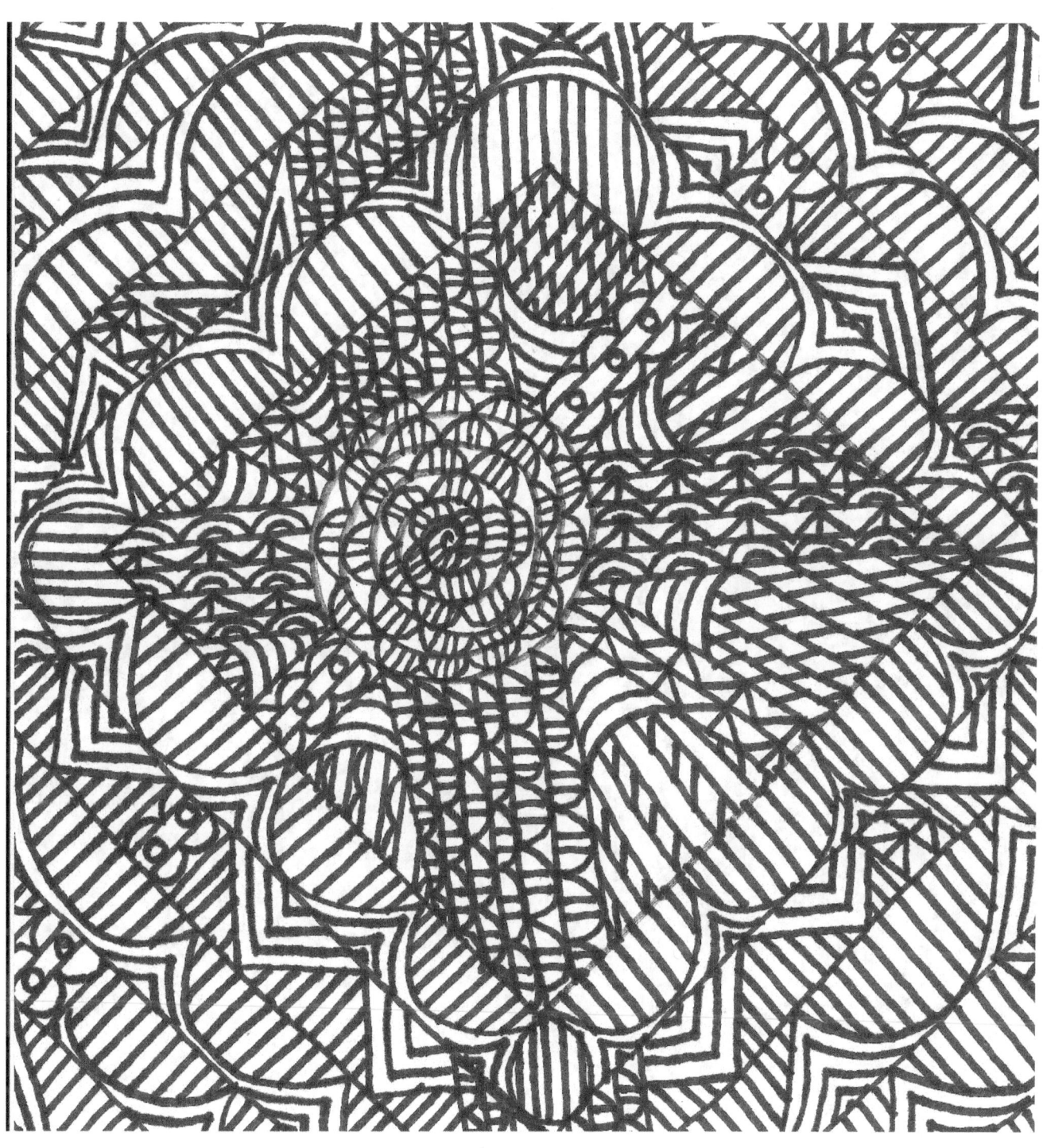

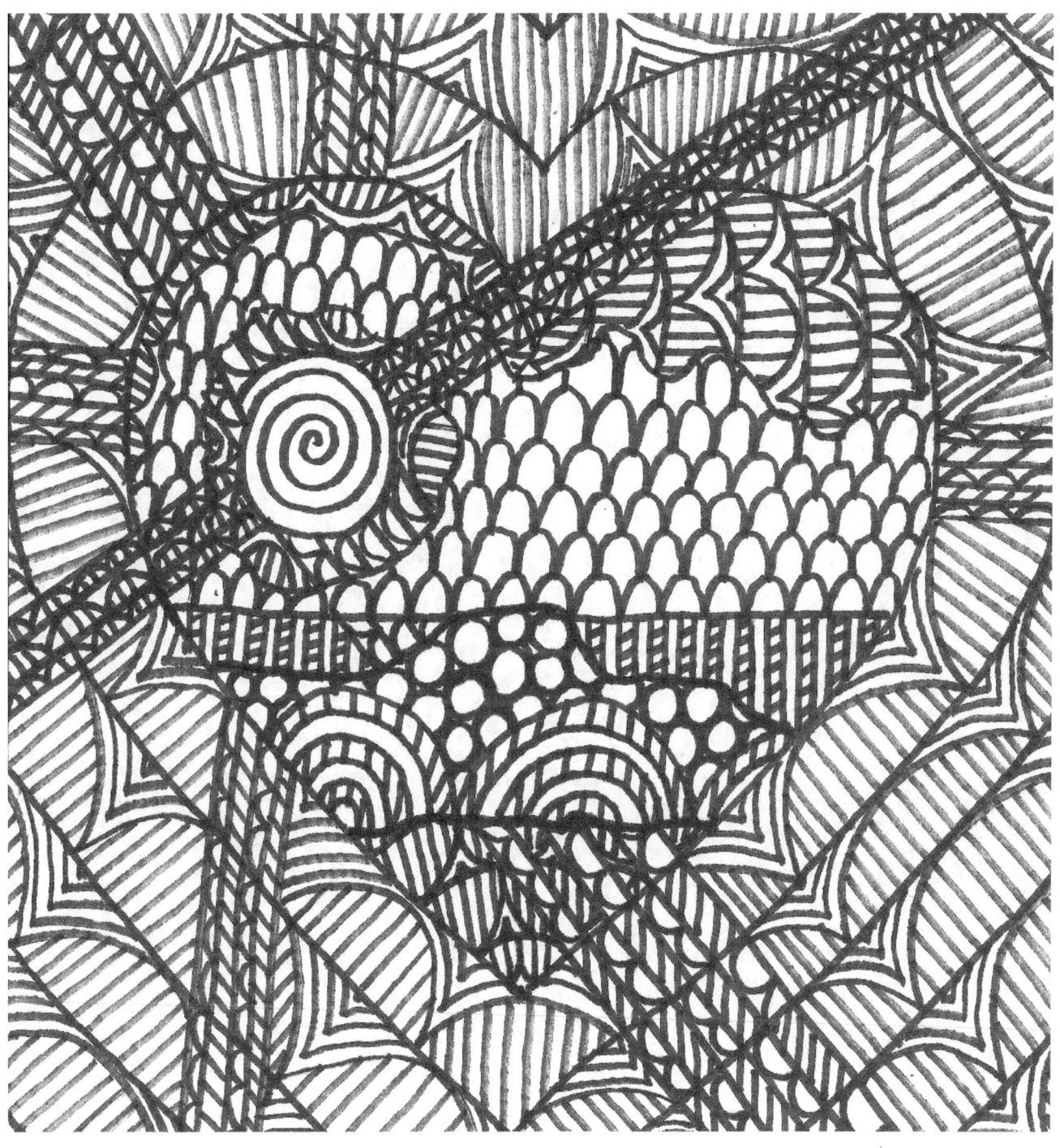

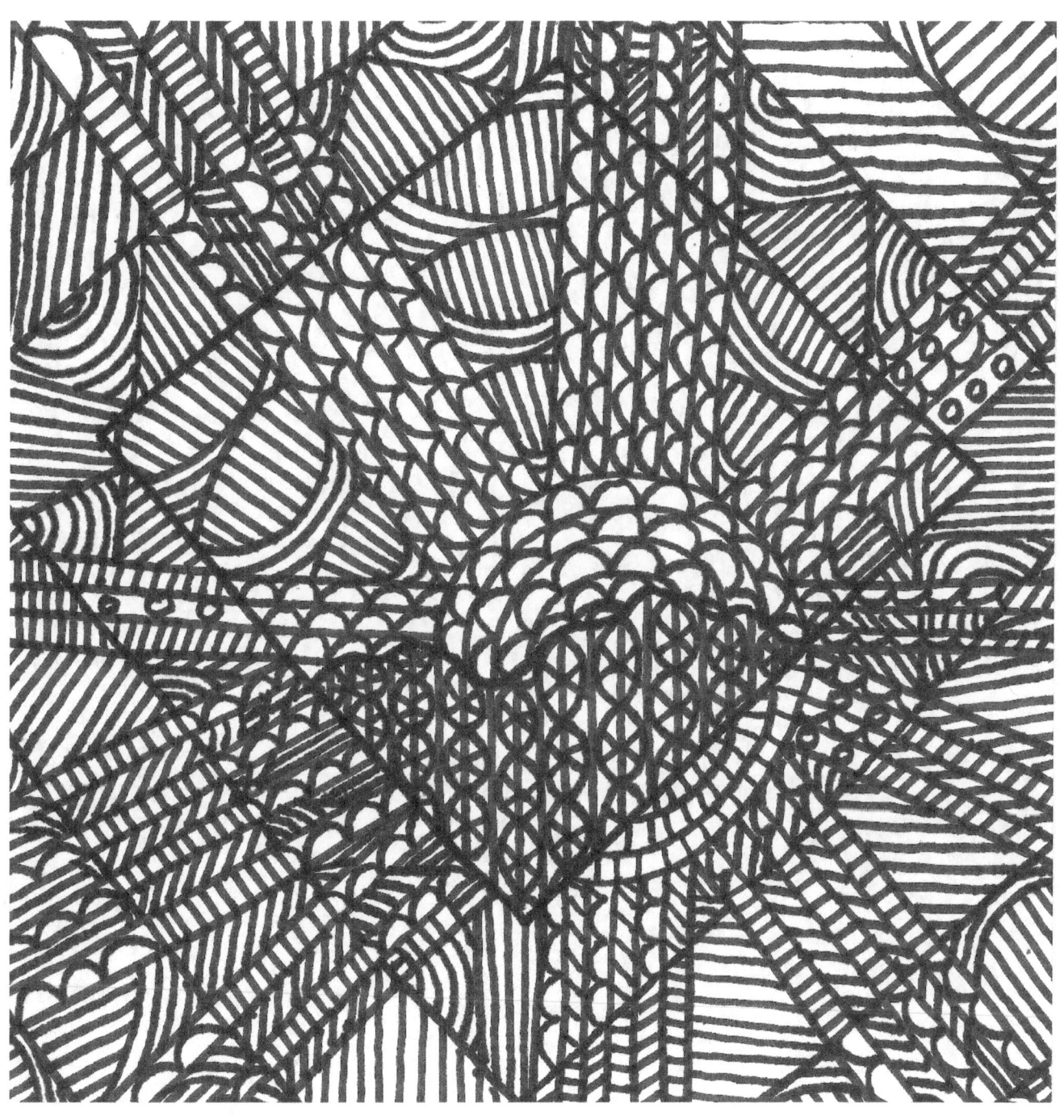

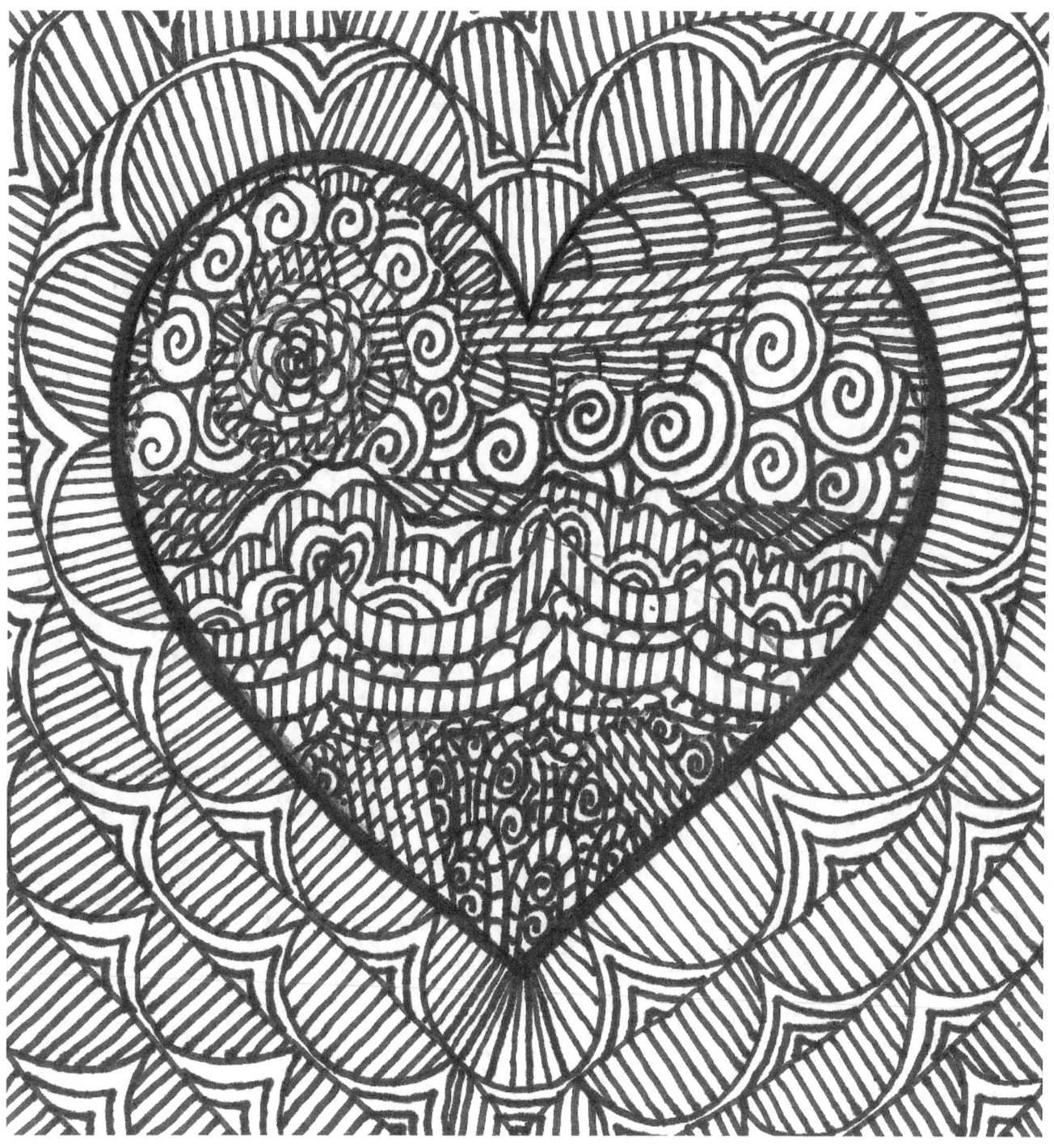

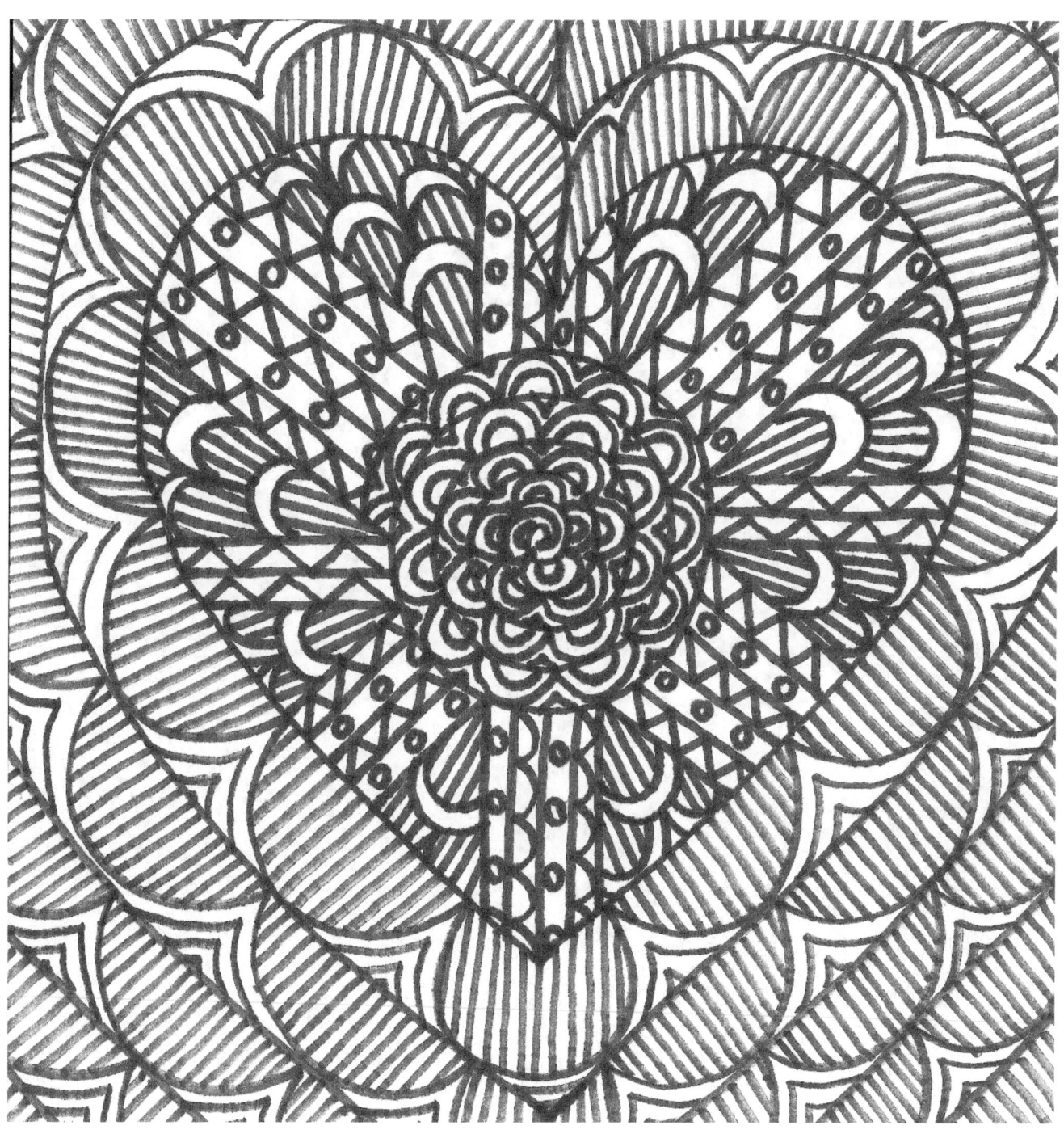

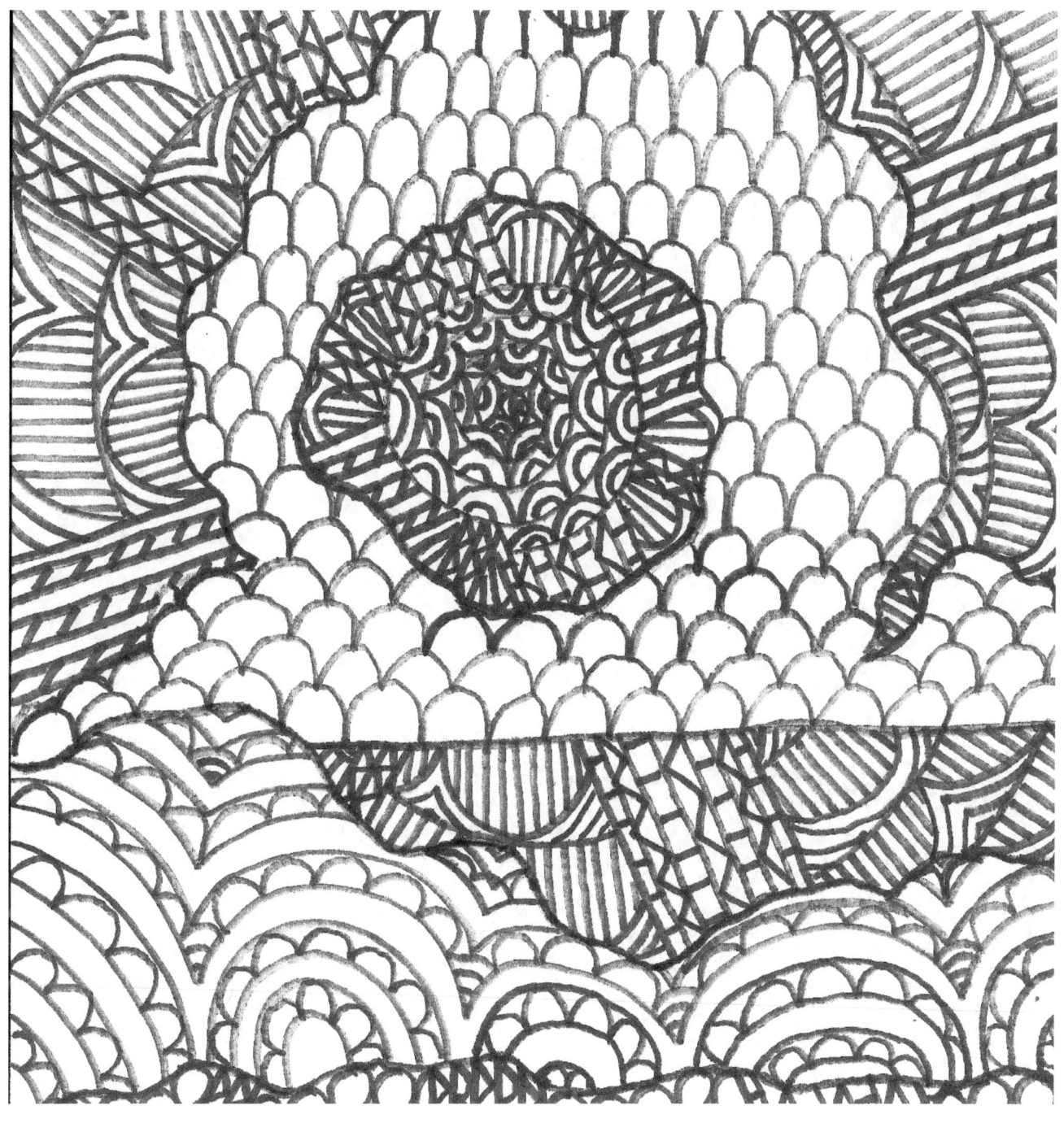

New Mexico Dreamscapes II

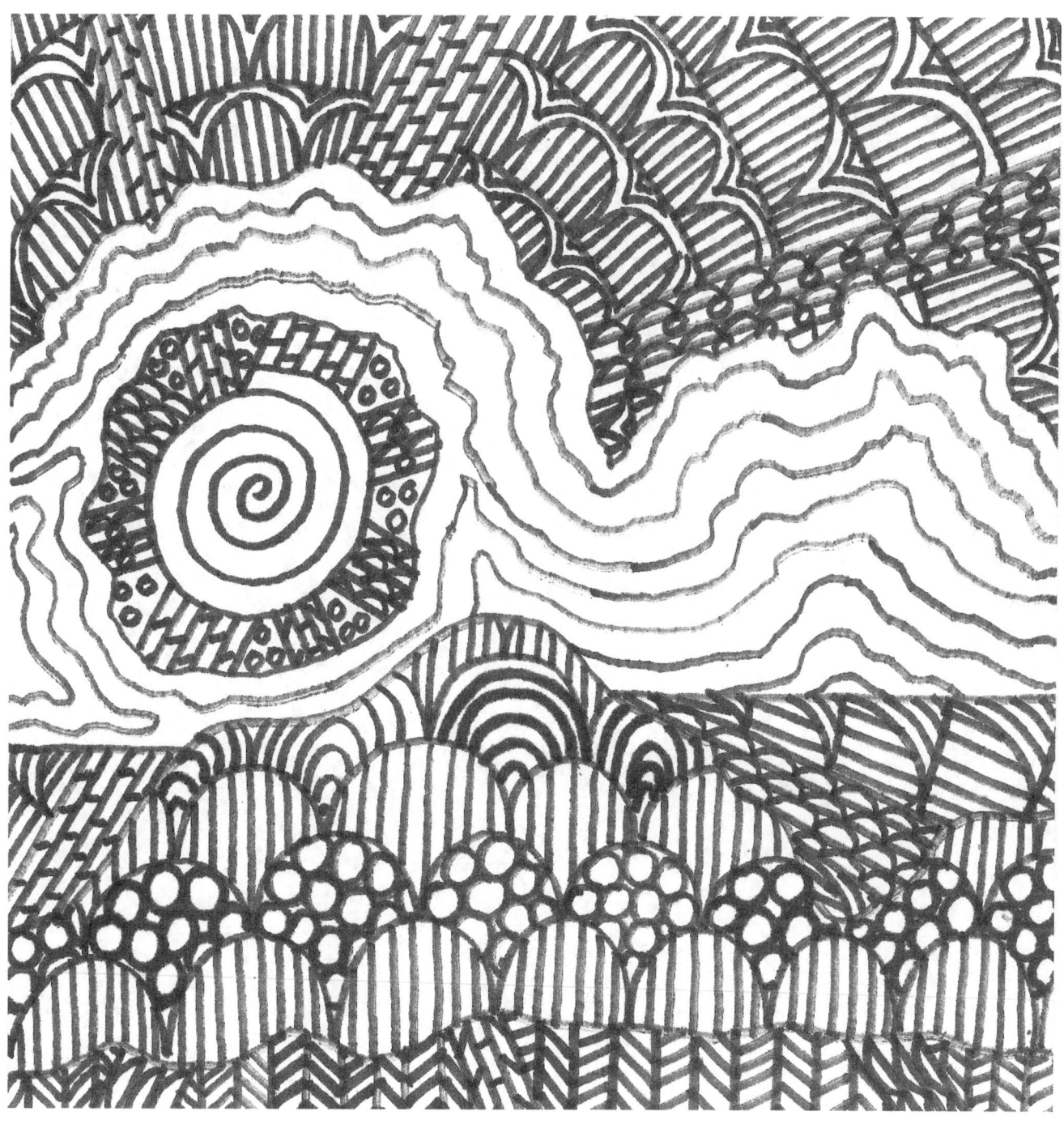

New Mexico Dreamscapes II

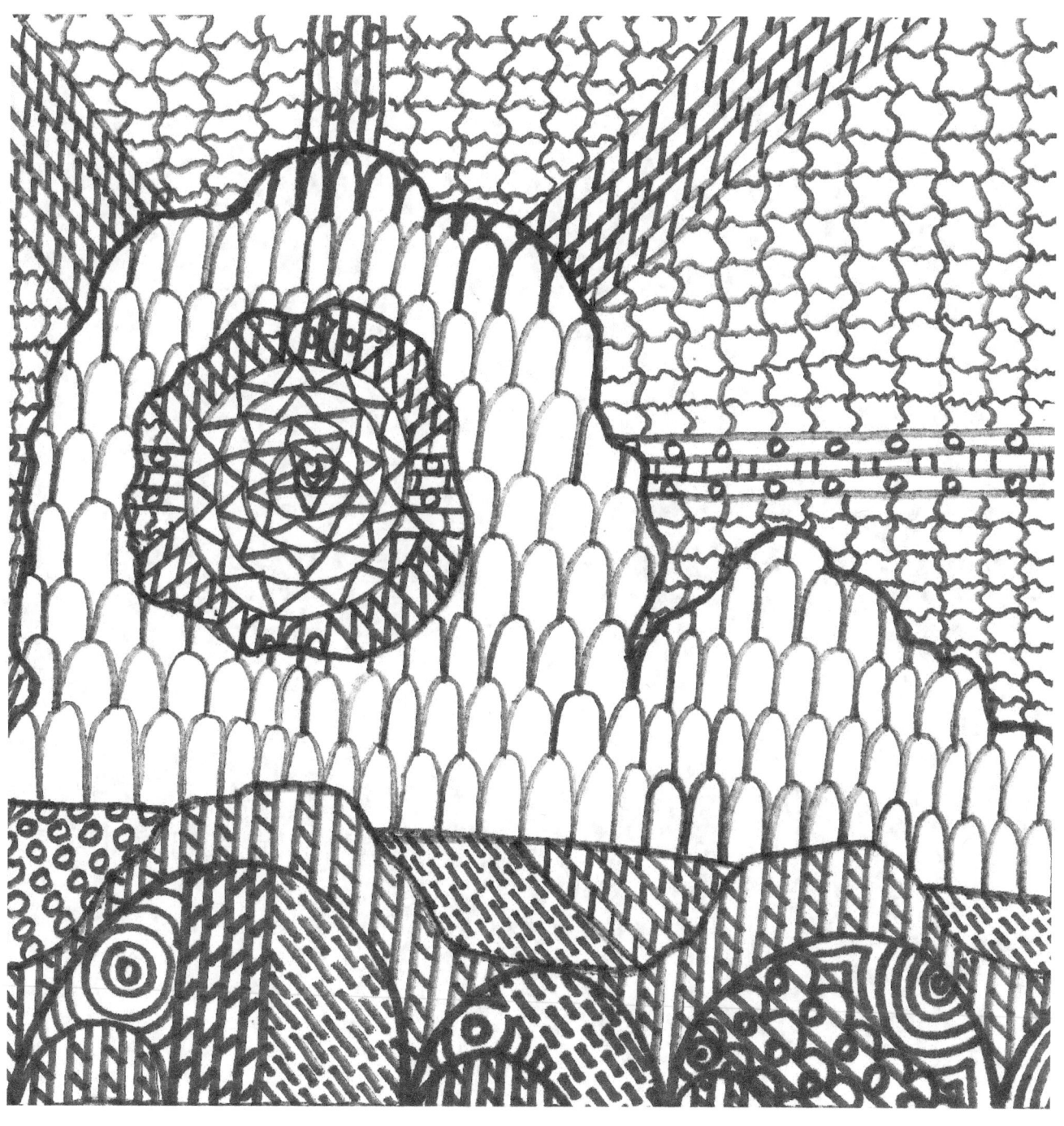

New Mexico Dreamscapes II

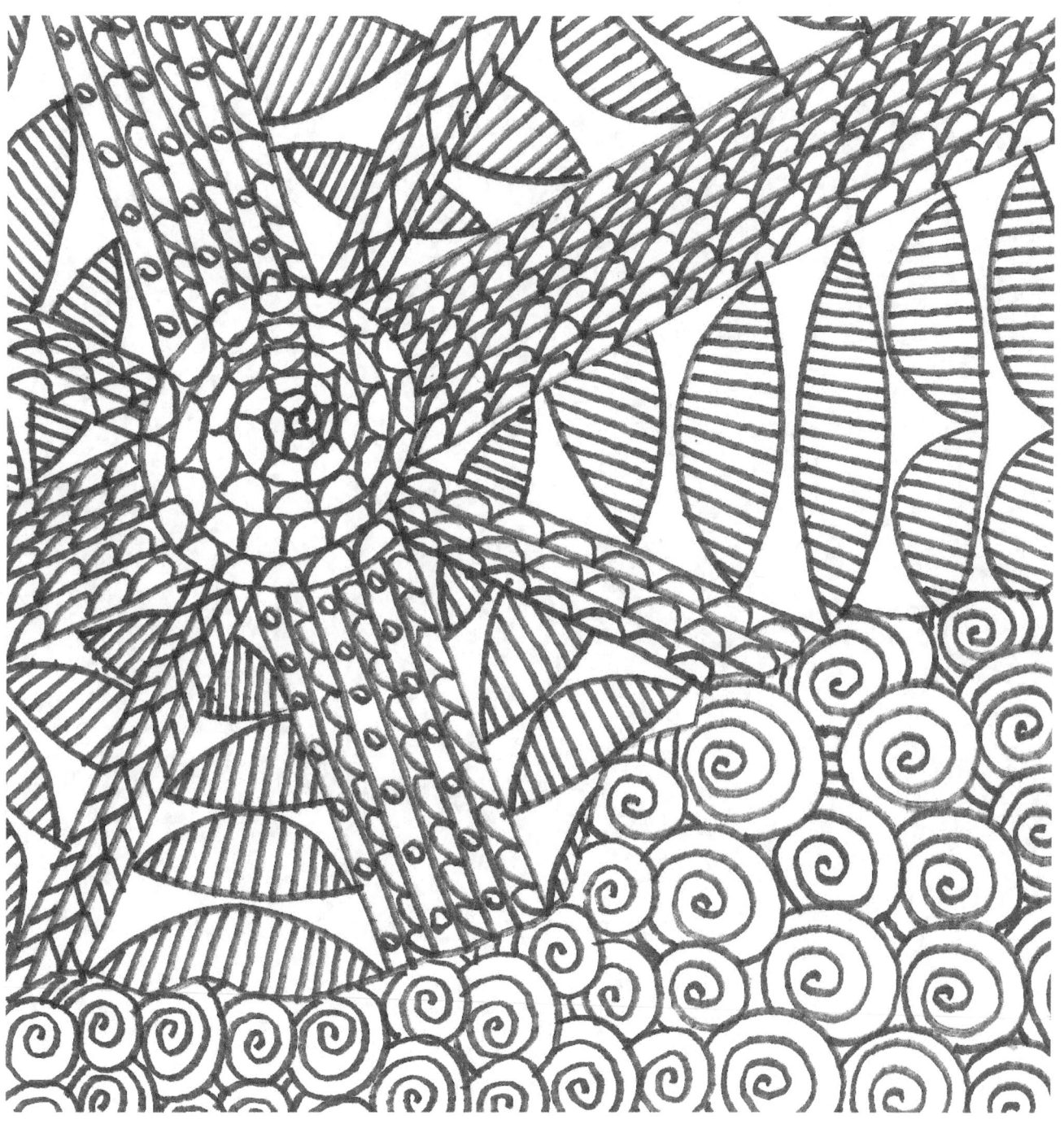

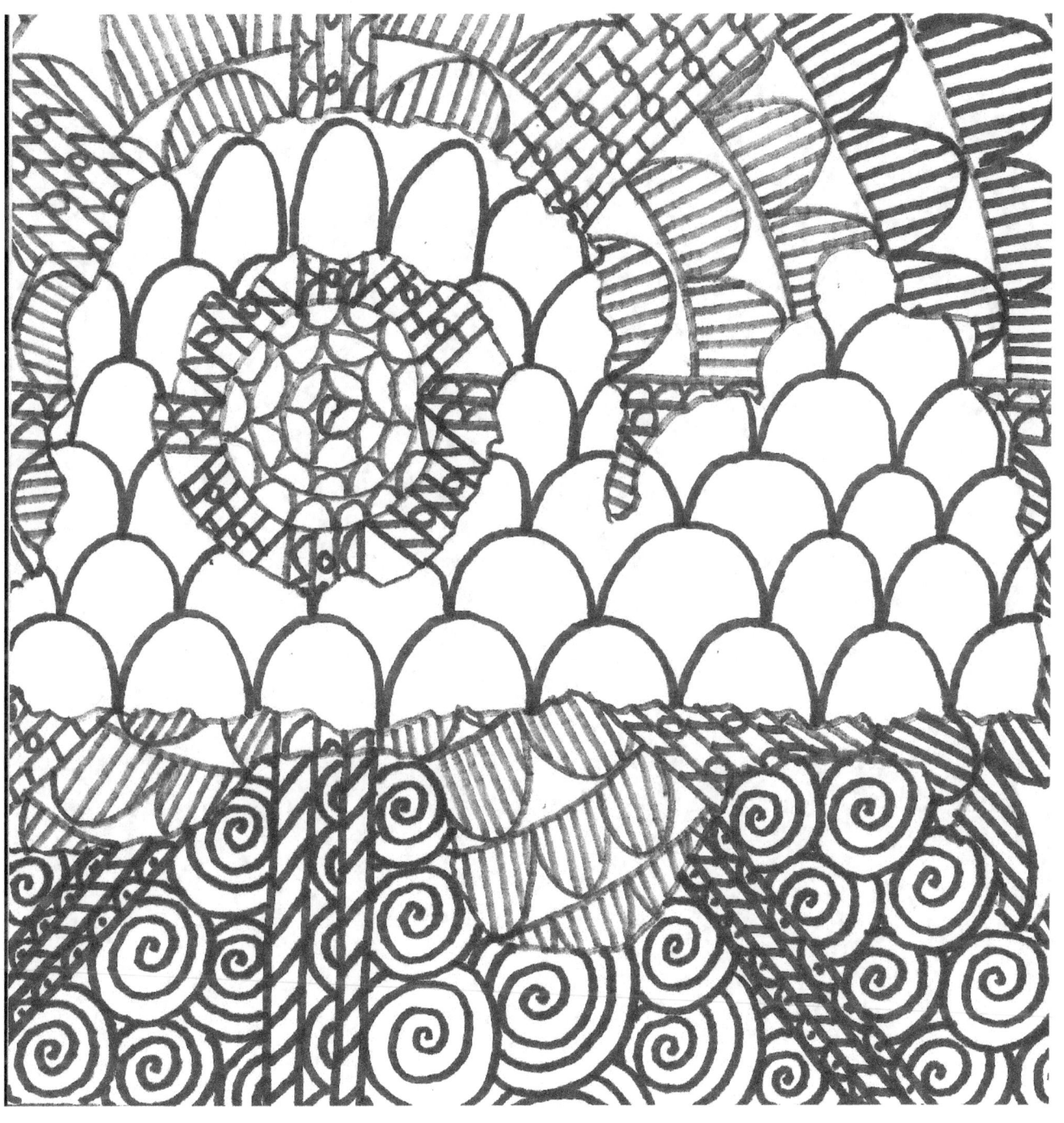

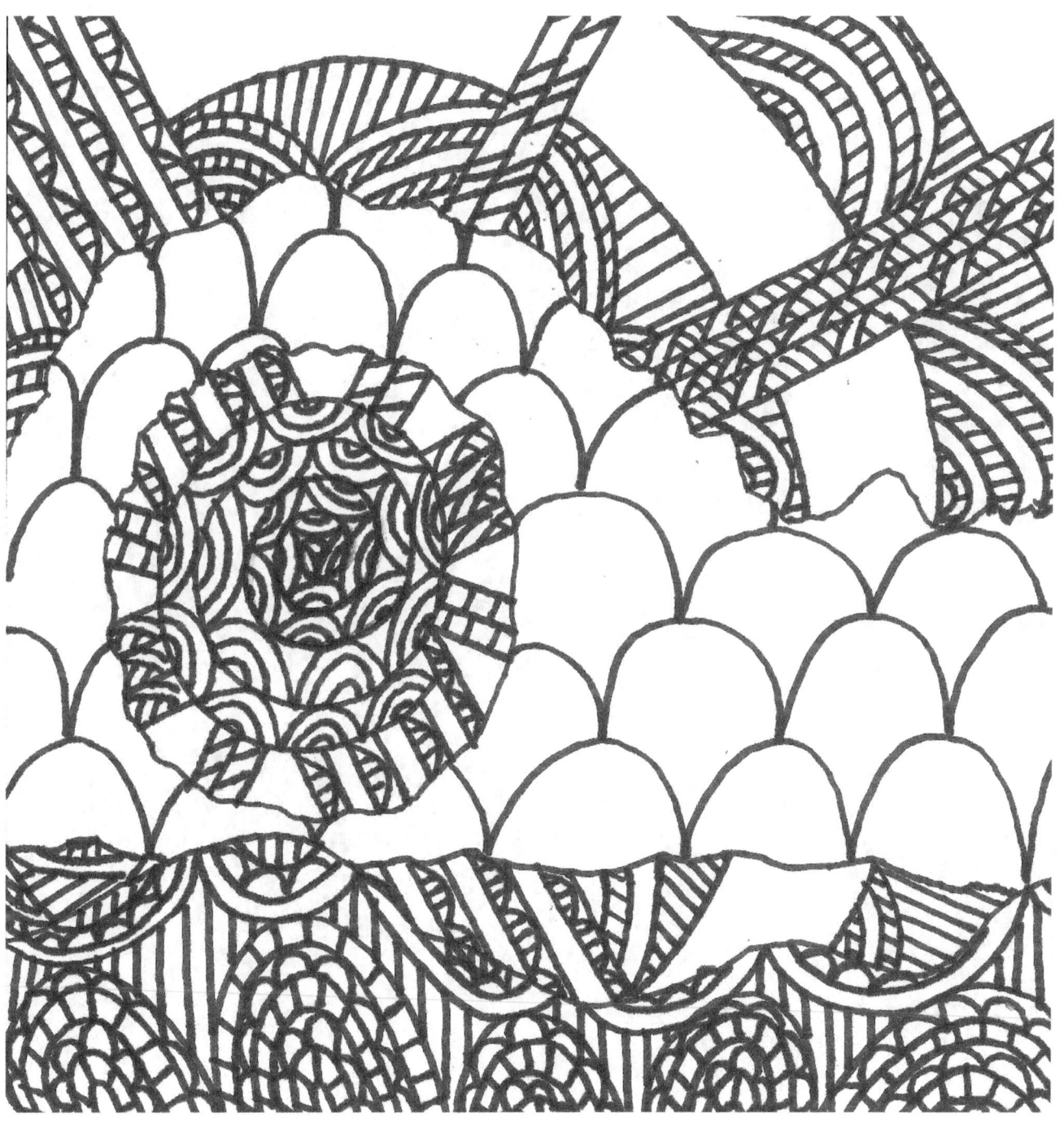

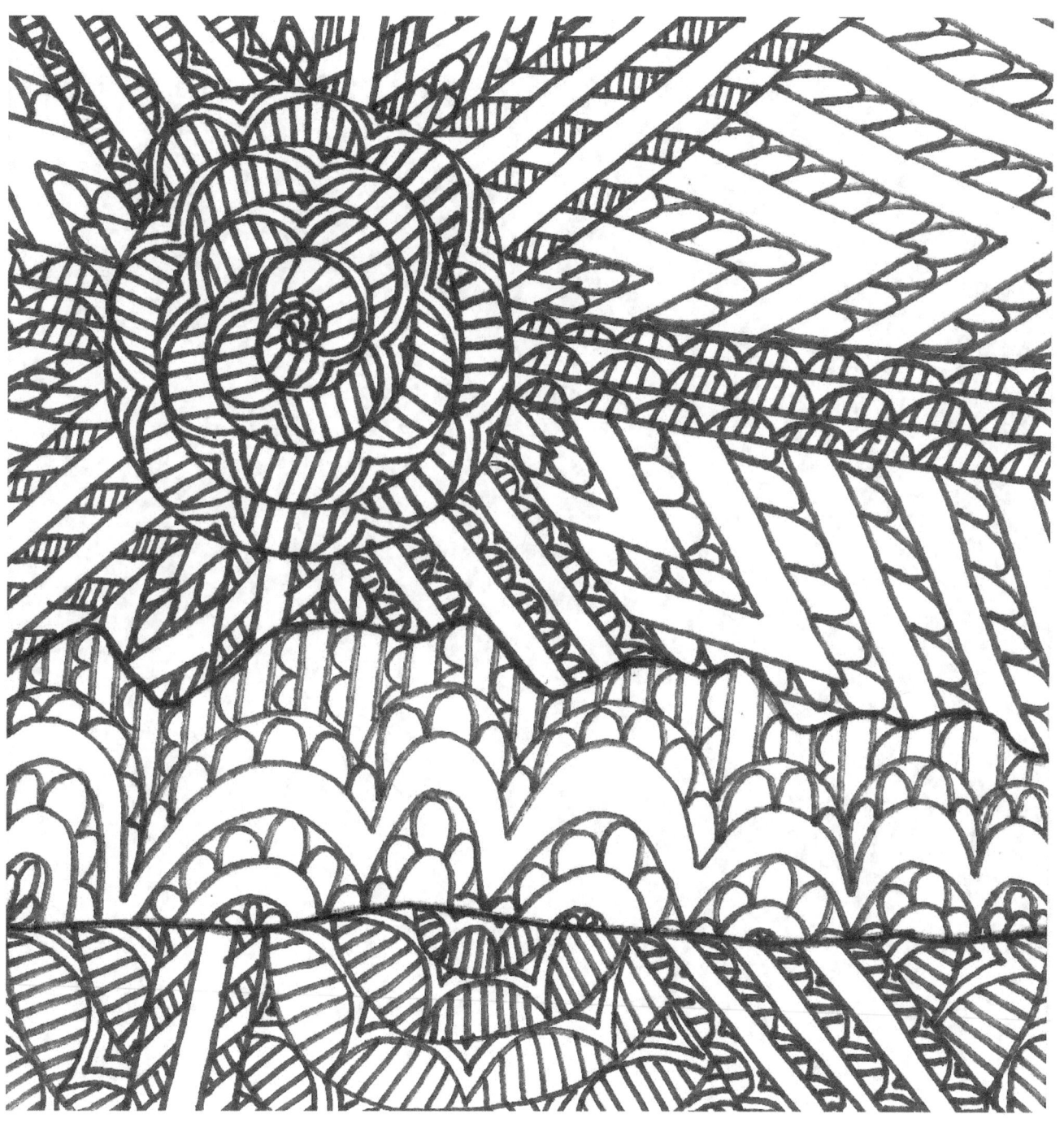

New Mexico Dreamscapes II

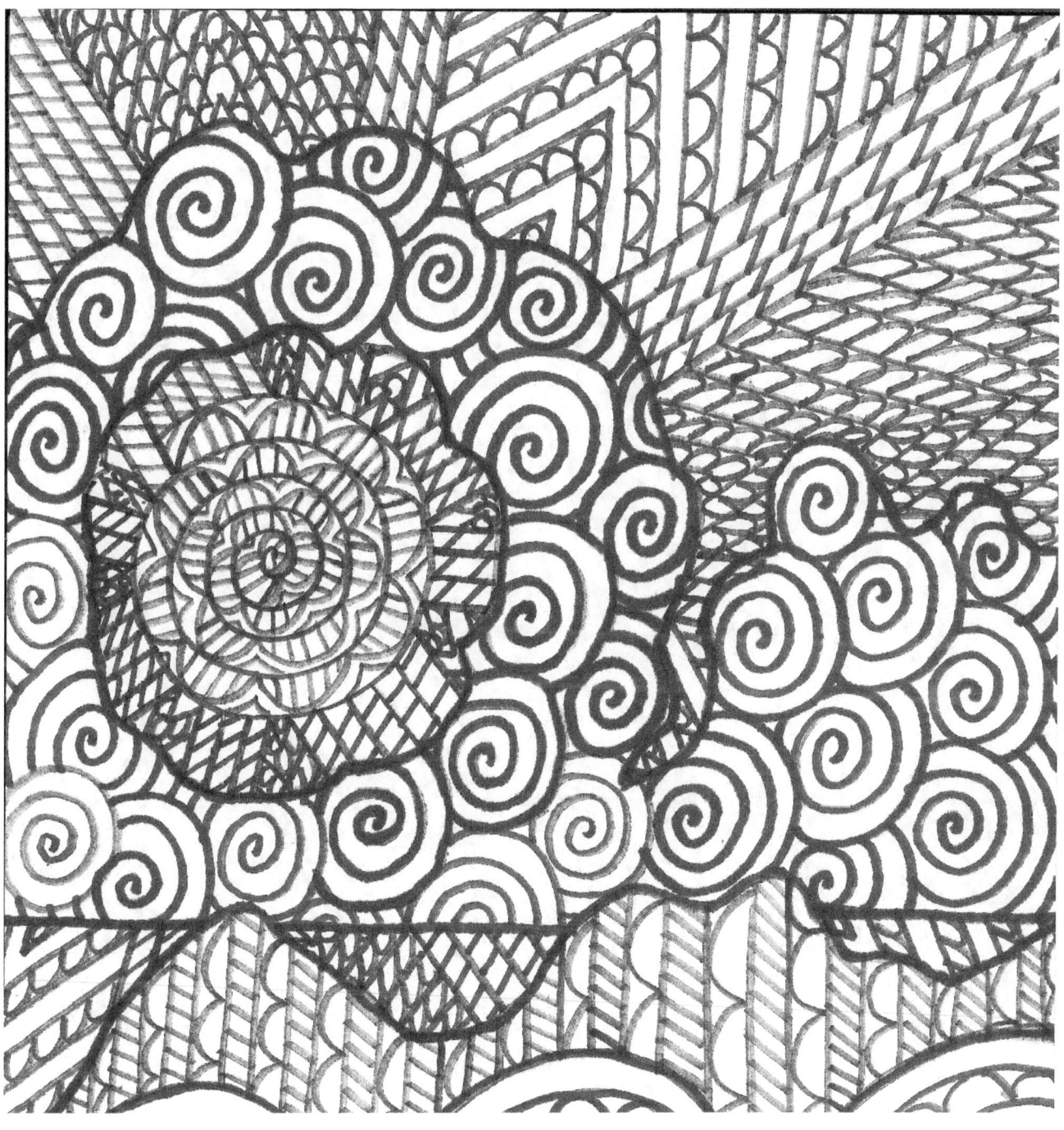

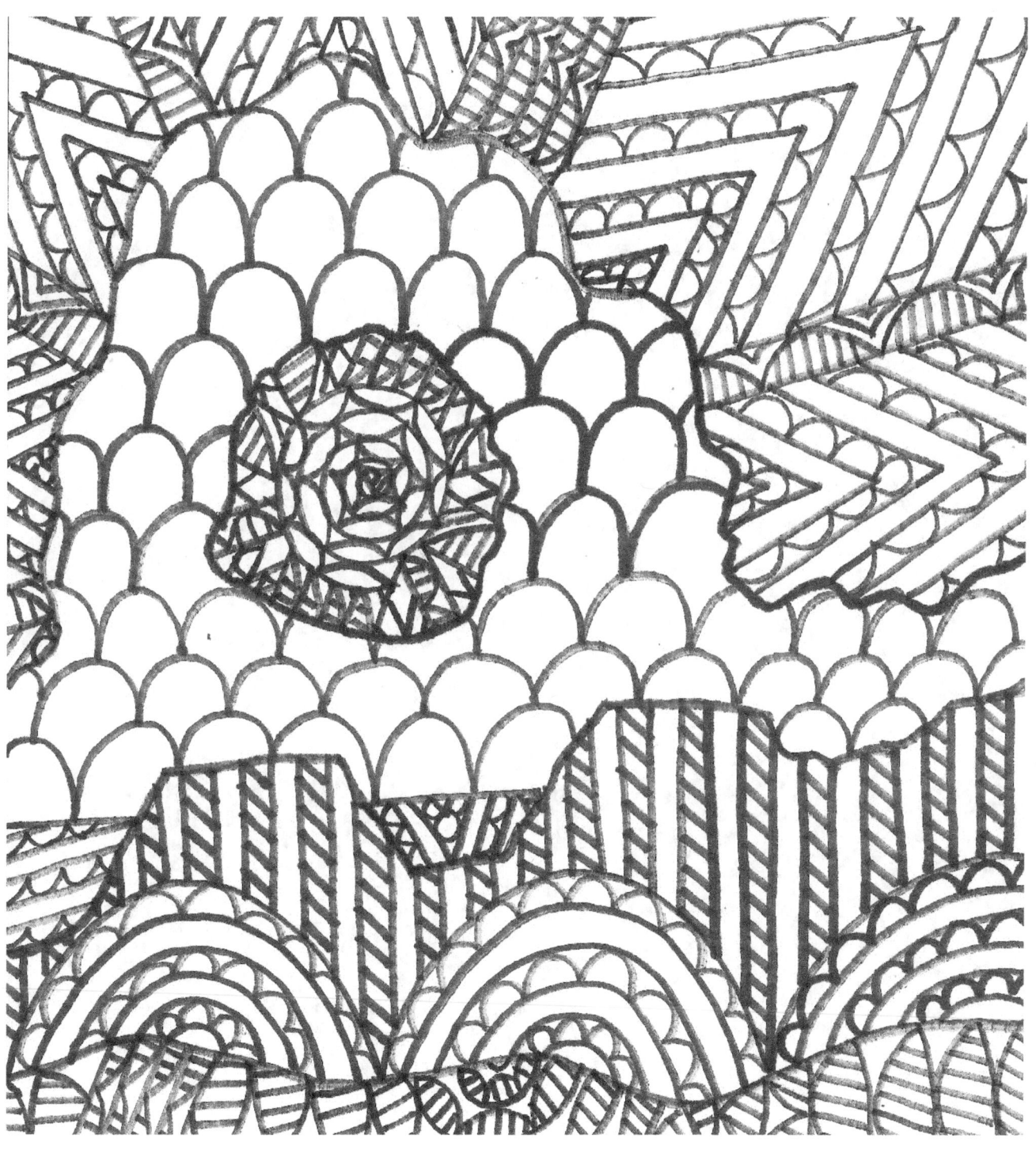

New Mexico Dreamscapes II

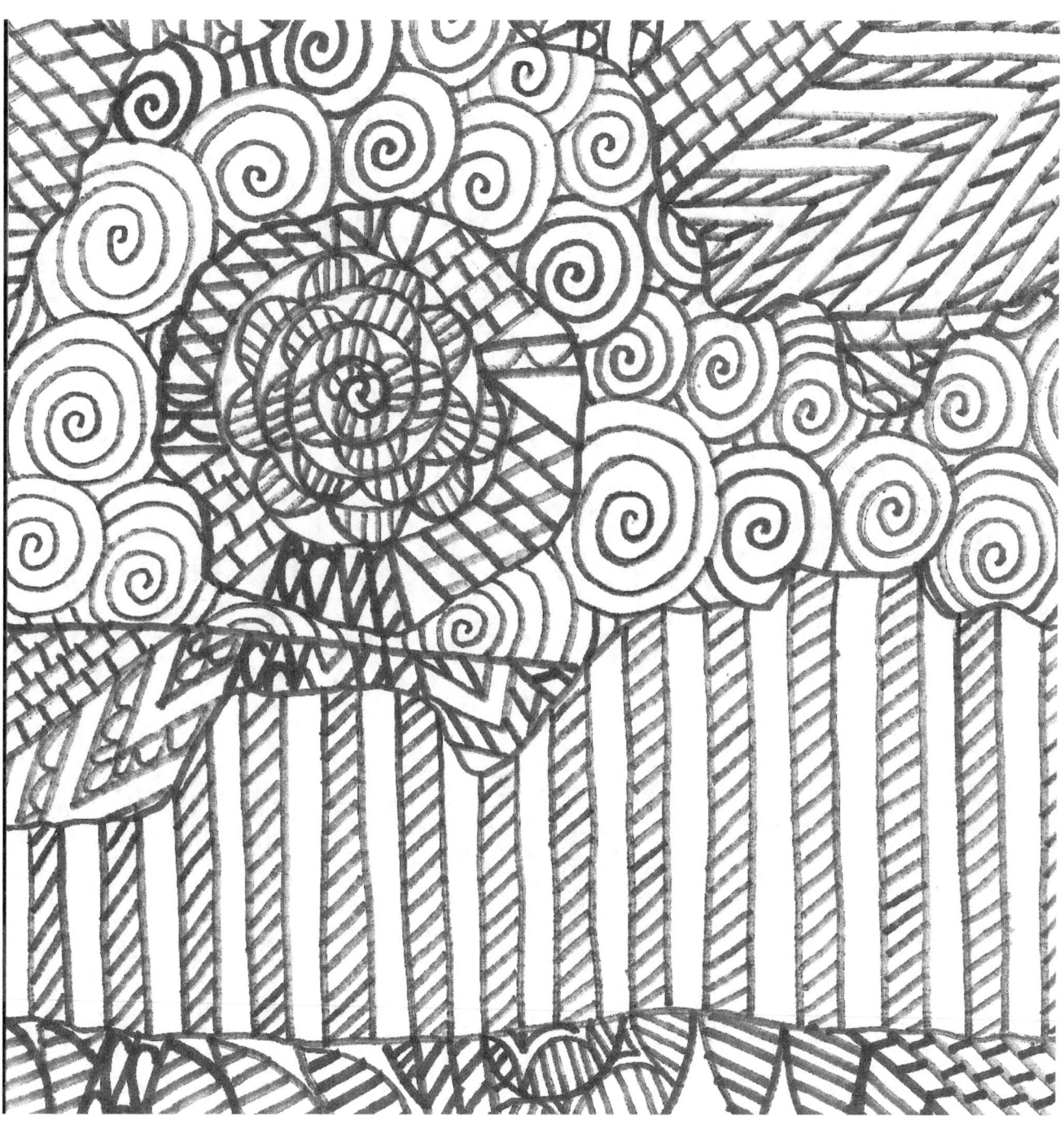

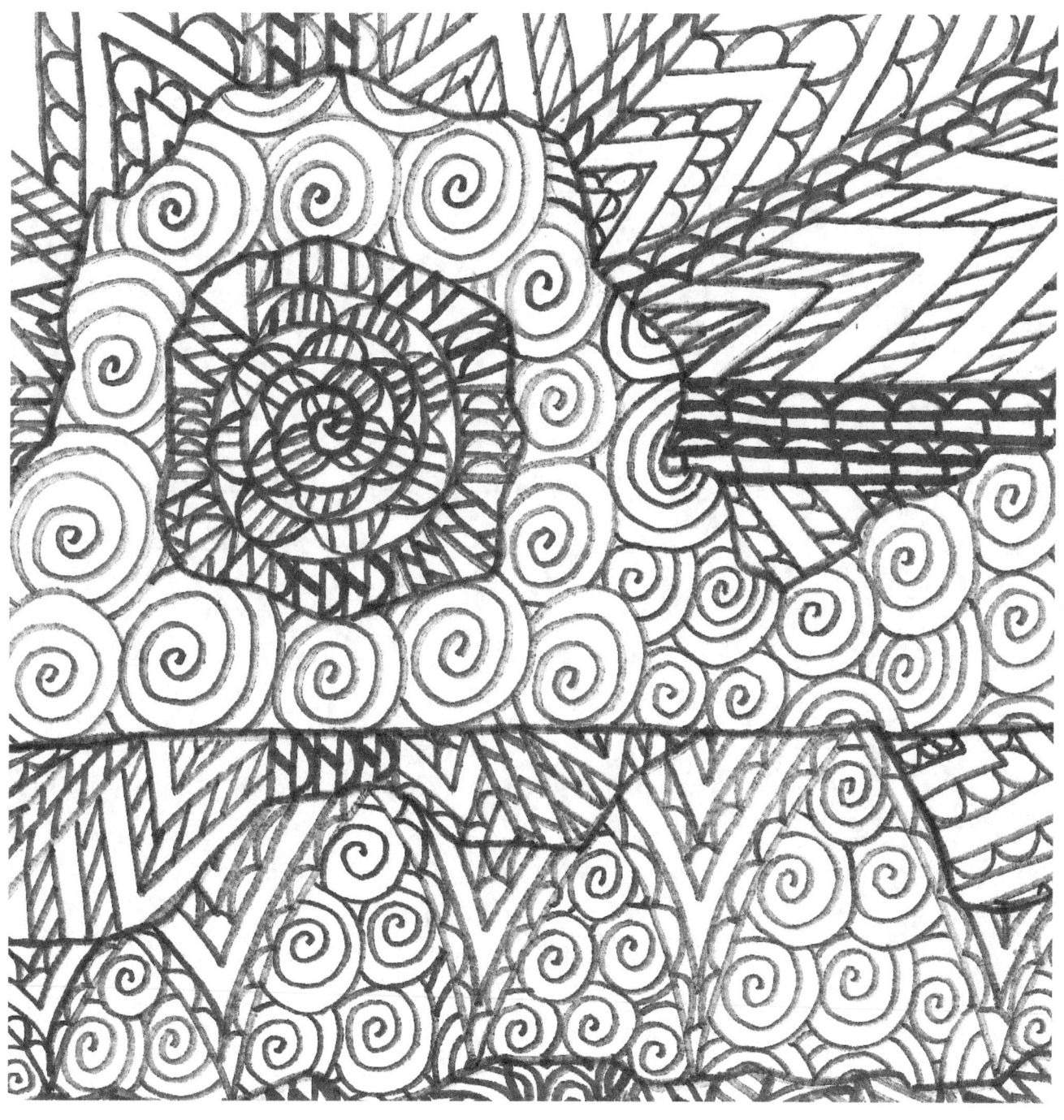

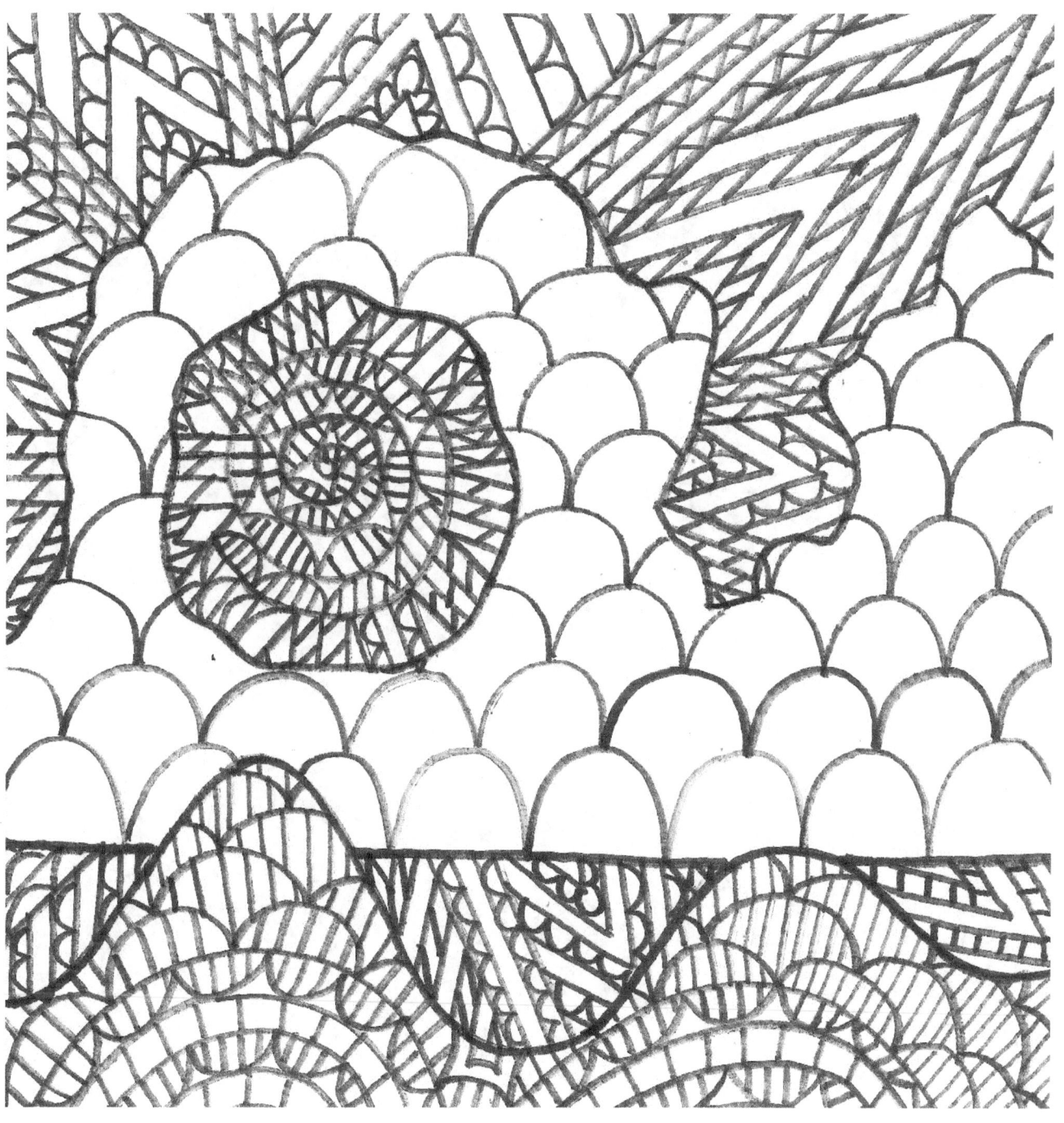

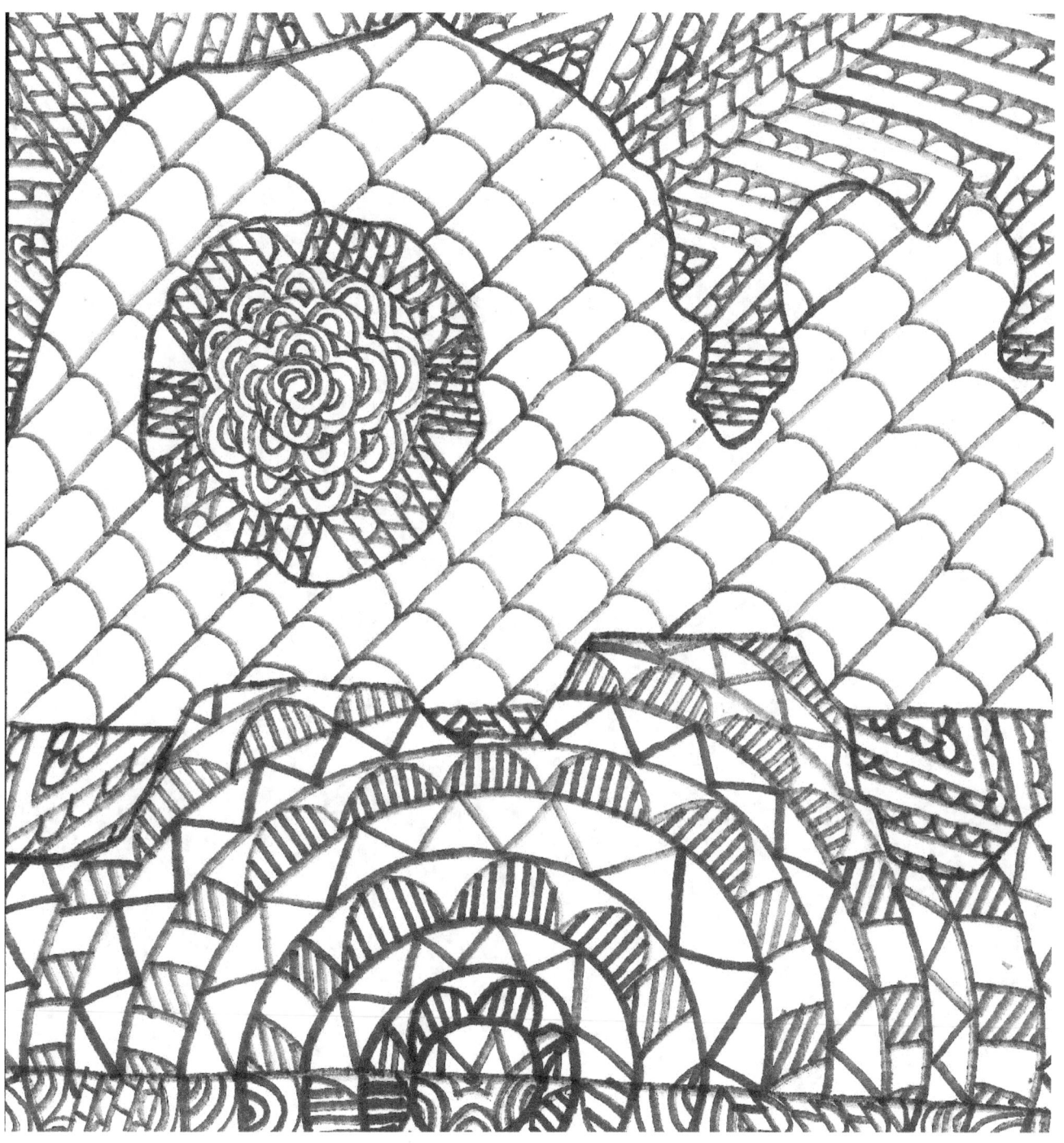

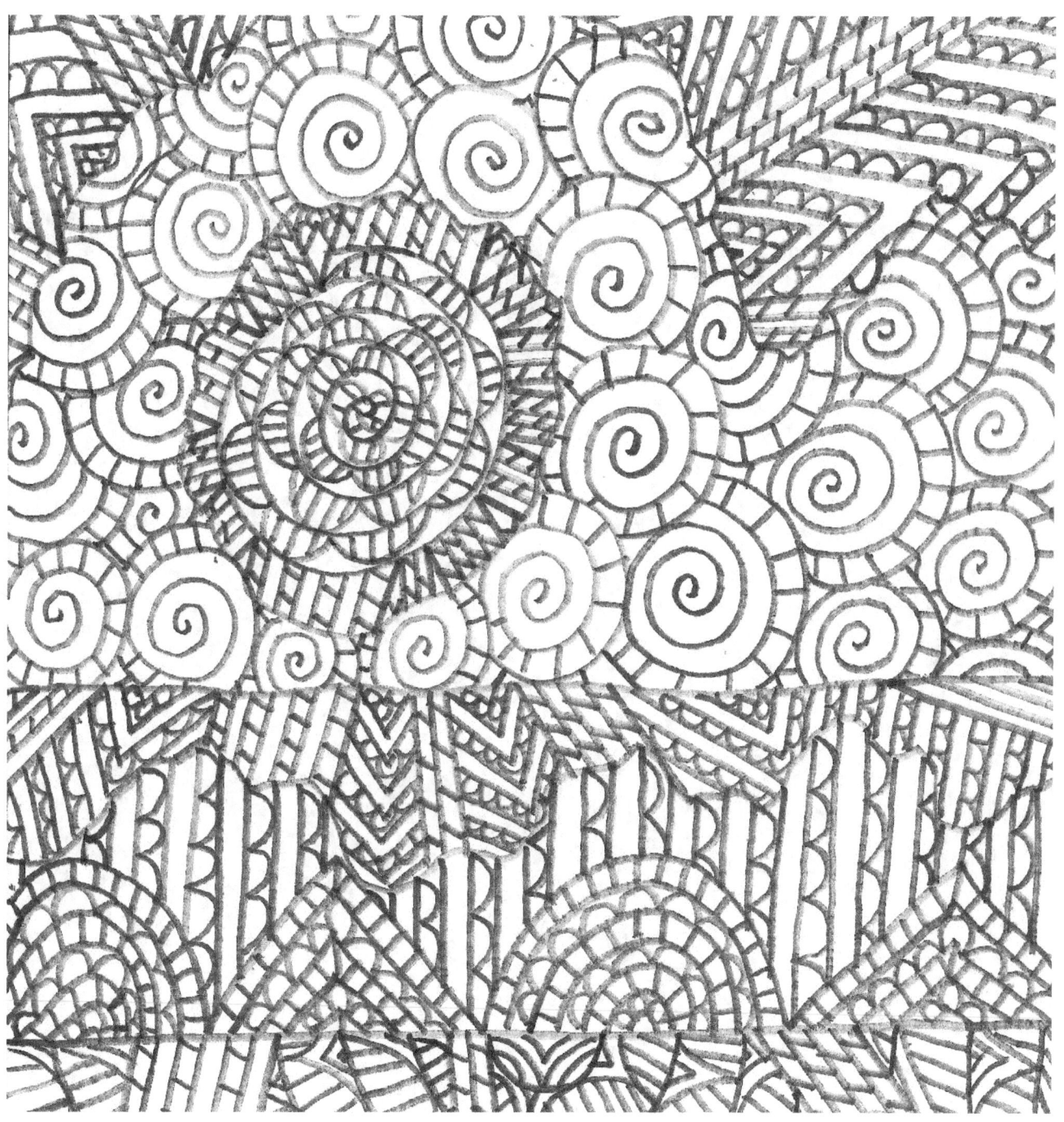

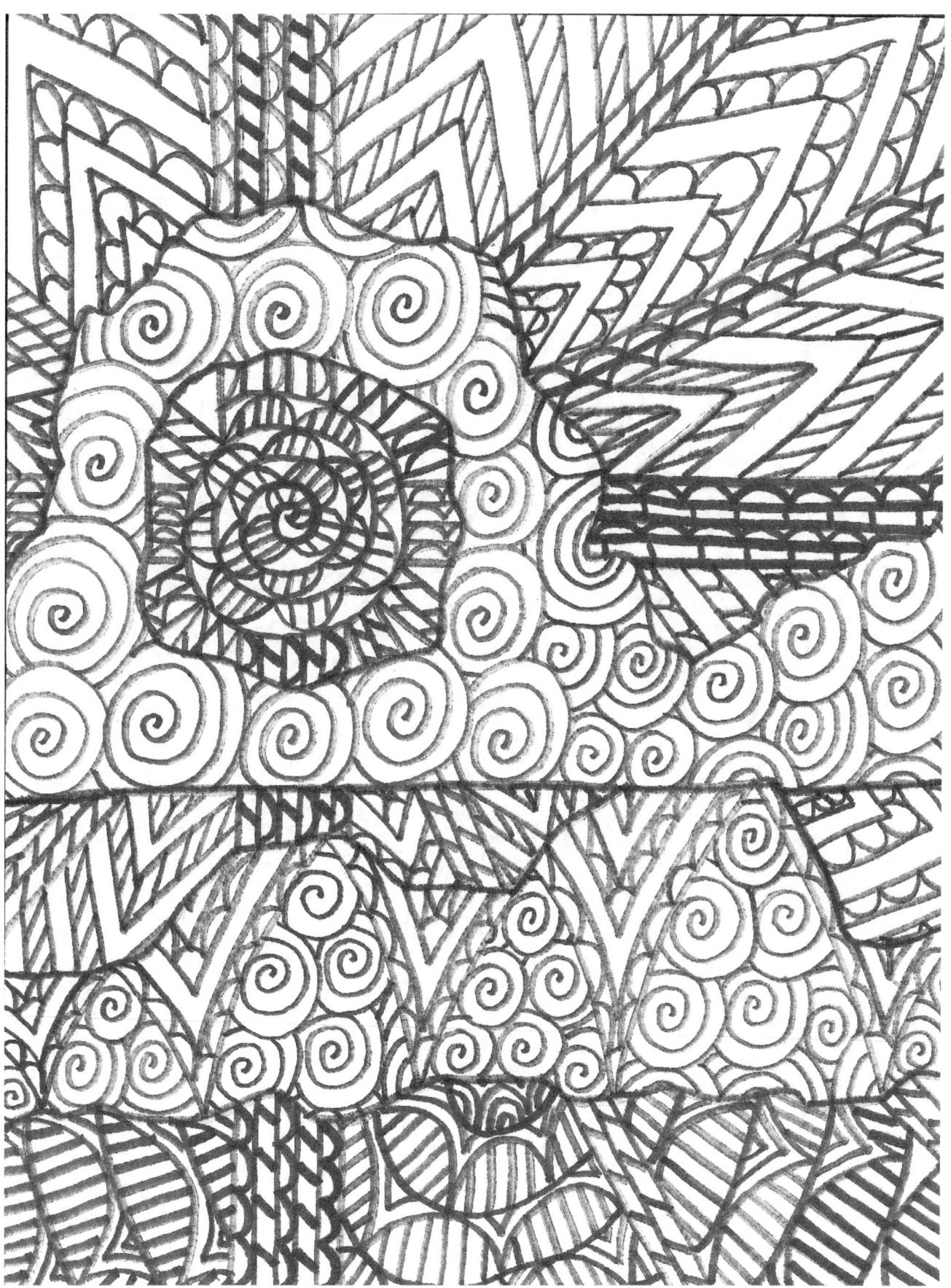

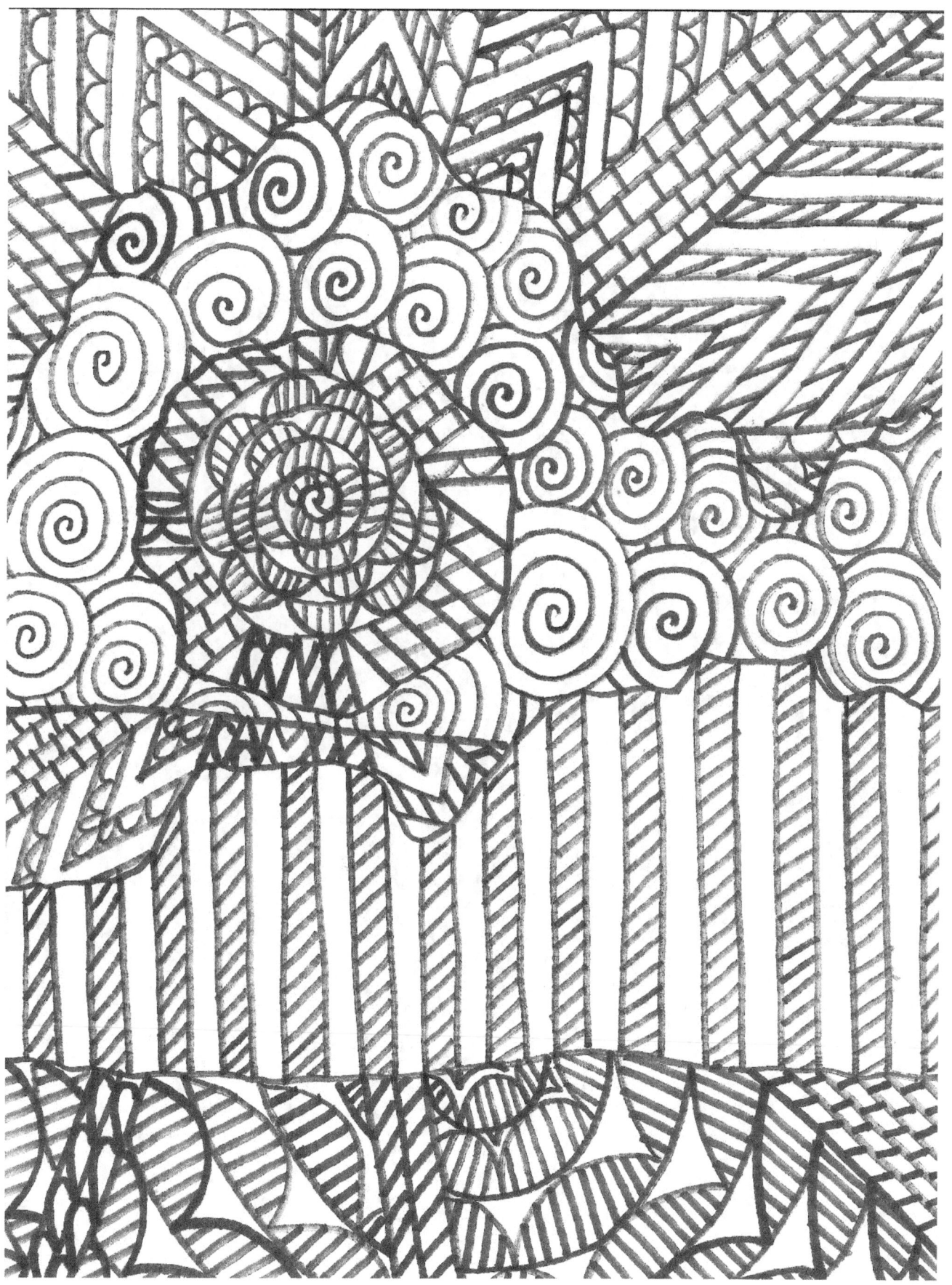

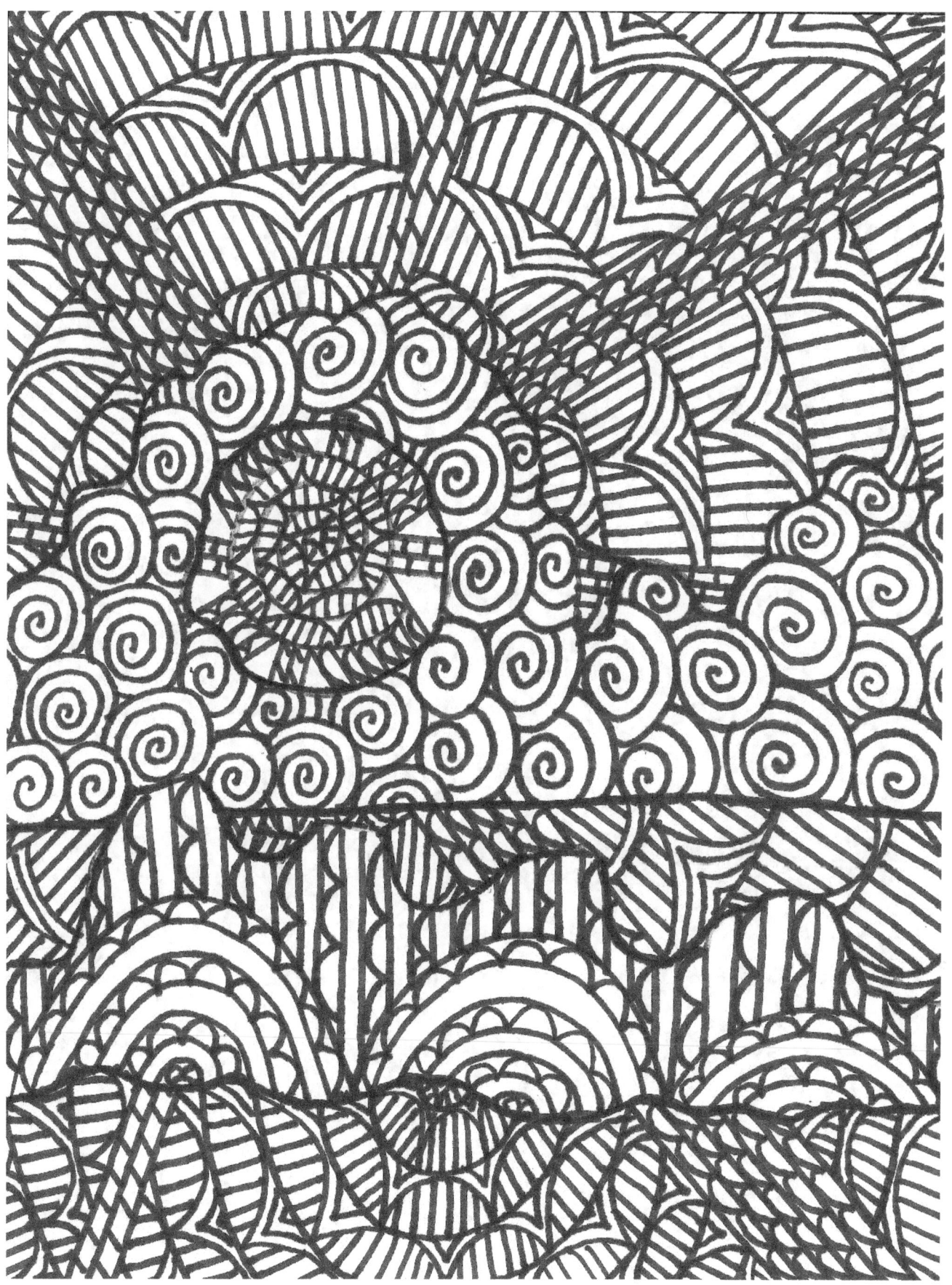

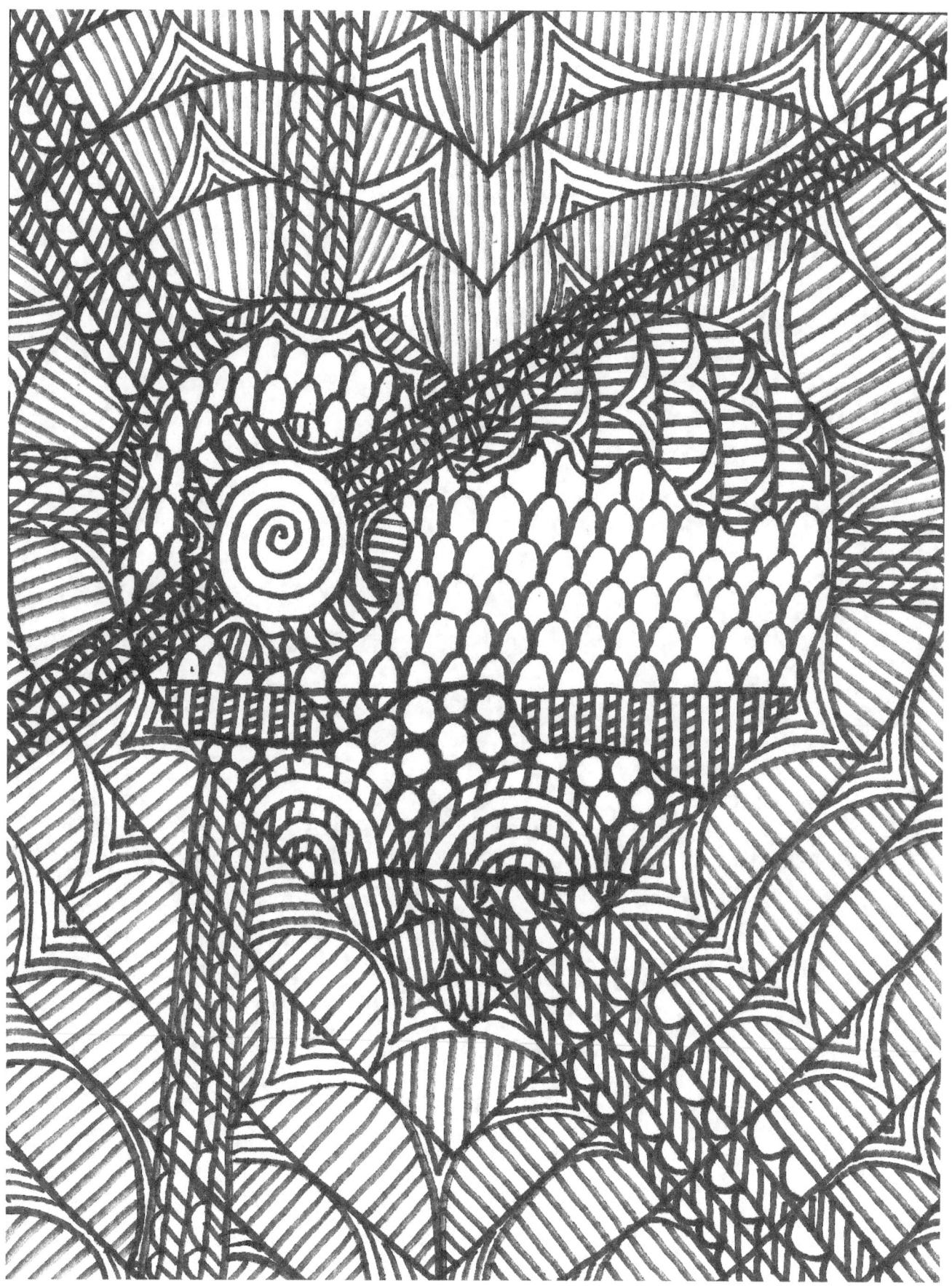

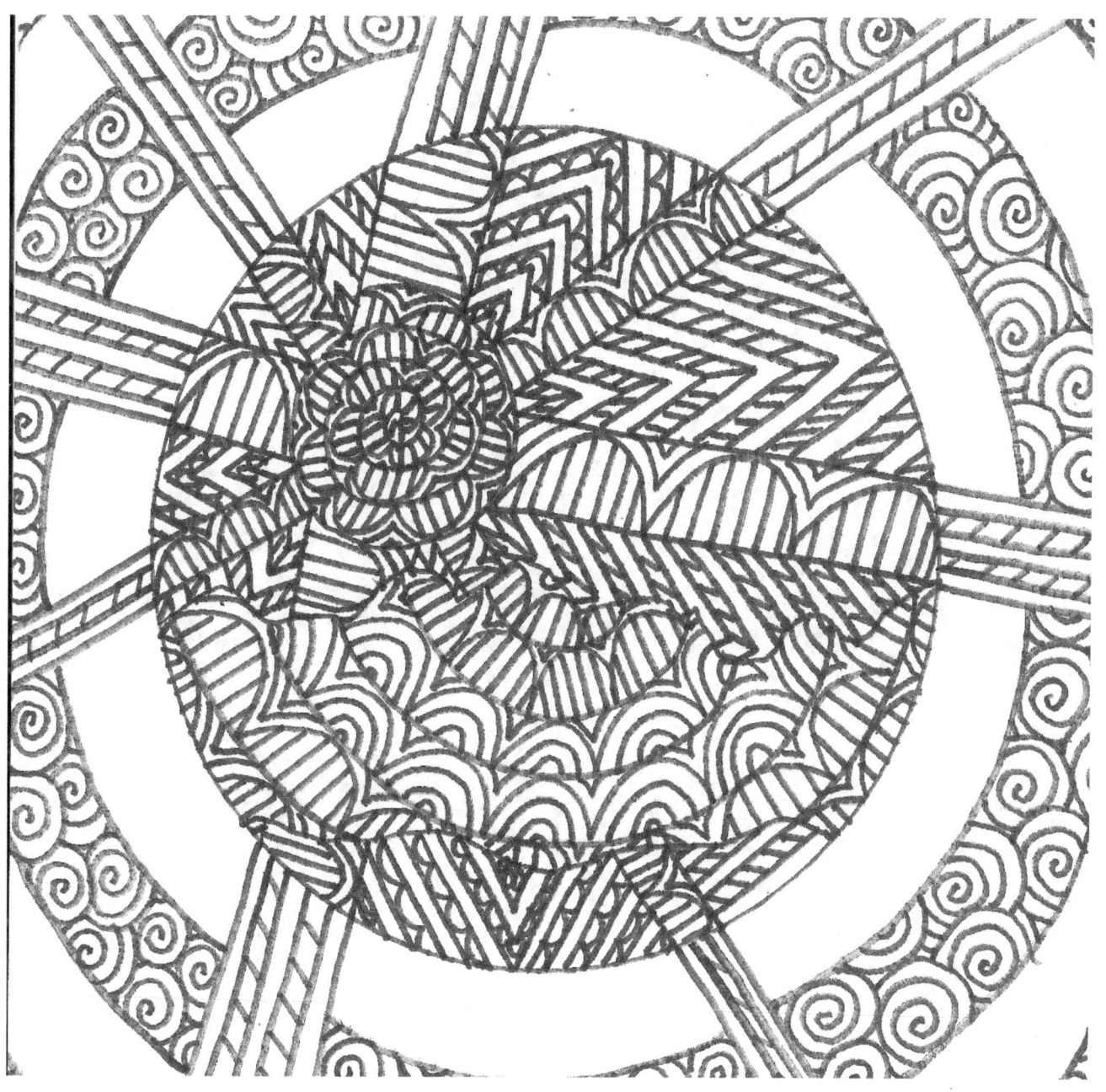

New Mexico Dreamscapes II

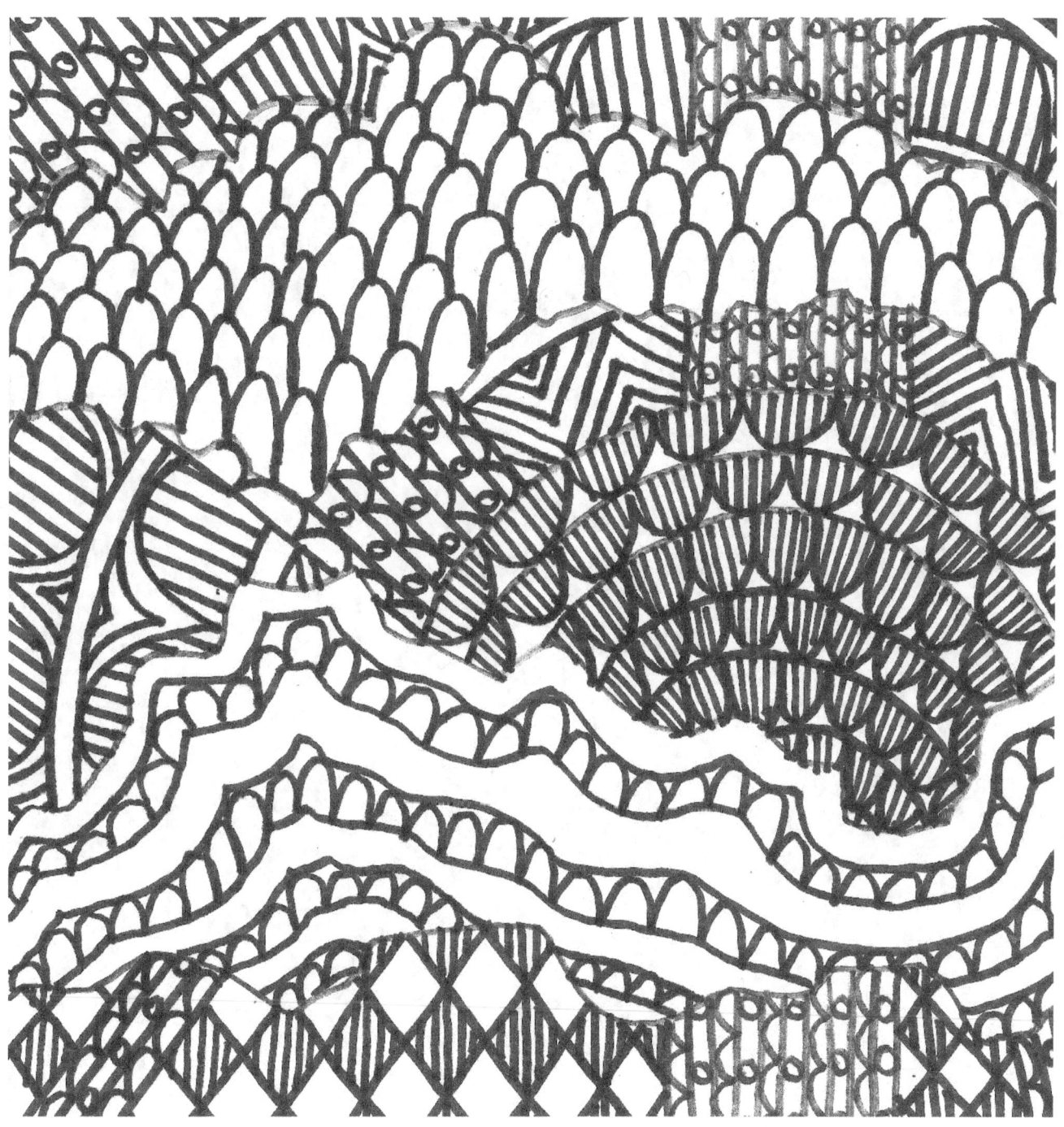

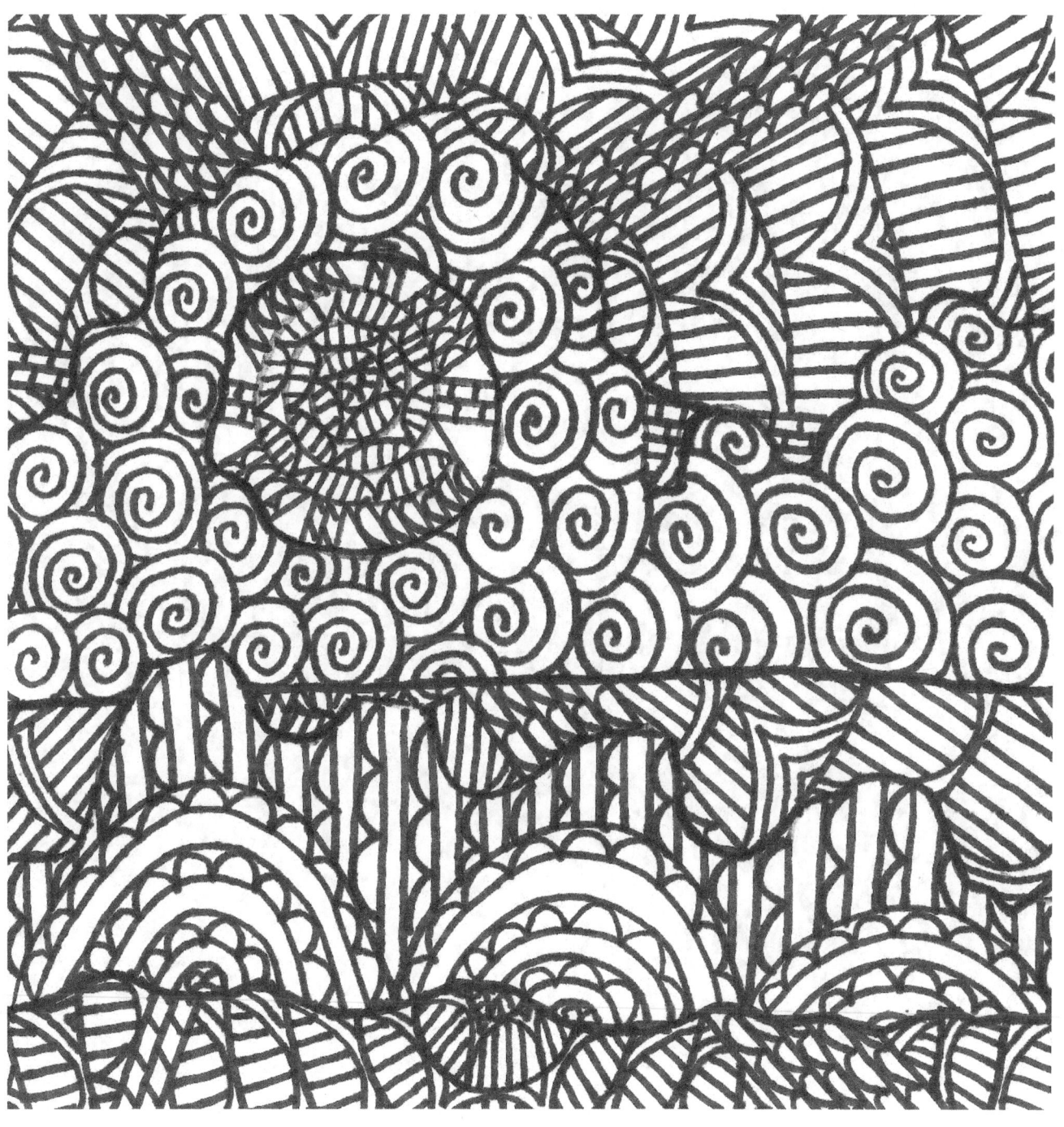

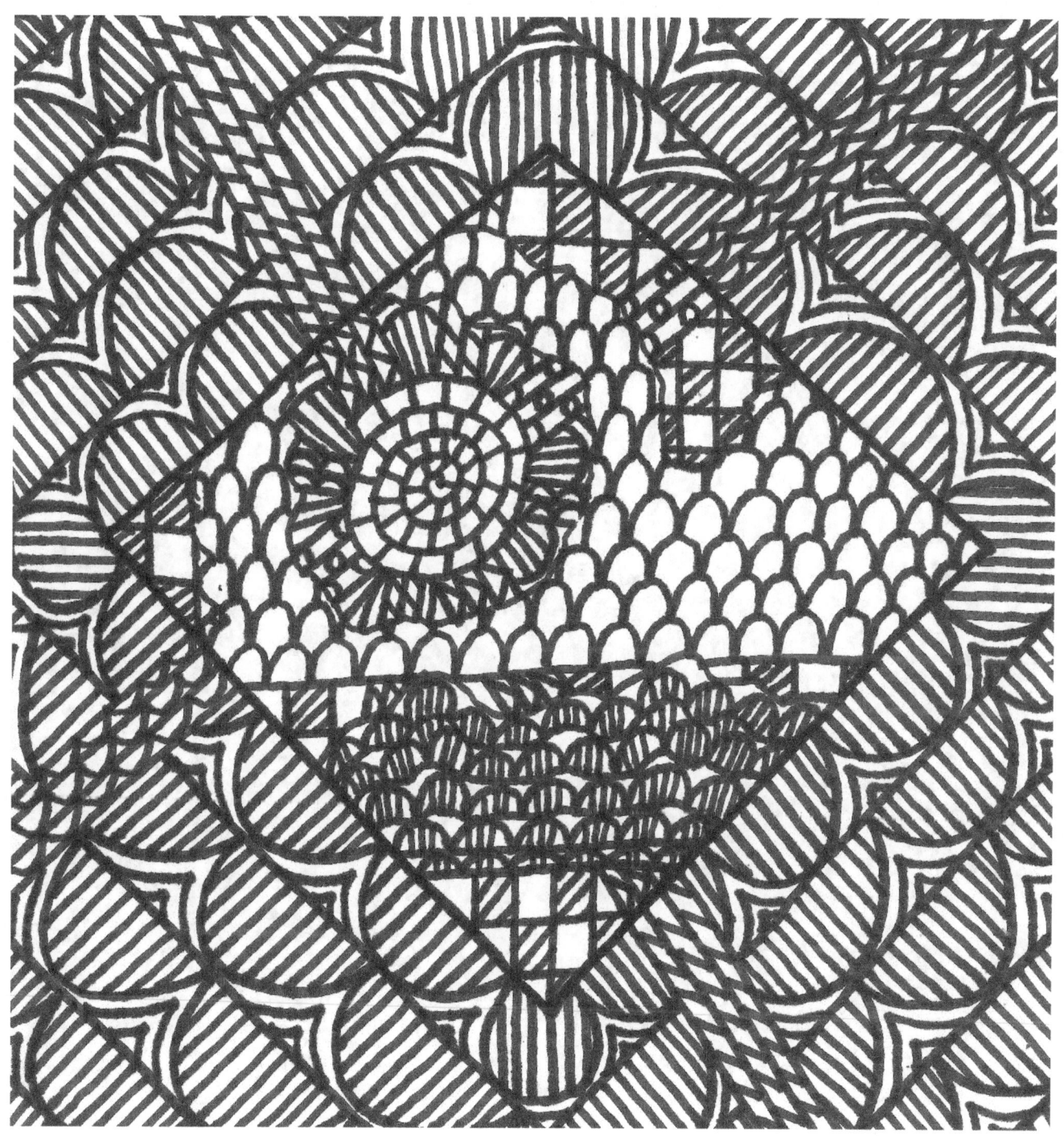

ABOUT THE AUTHOR

BOBBY J. JONES WAS BORN AT REESE AIR FORCE BASE HOSPITAL IN LUBBOCK, TEXAS IN 1966. BOBBY'S FAMILY MOVED TO FORT WORTH, TEXAS IN 1968. JONES IS THE YOUNGEST SON OF TWO DAUGTHERS AND TWO SONS.

HIS FATHER TONEY JONES WORKED FOR GENERAL DYNAMICS AS AN INDUSTRIAL ENGINEER IN THE ESTIMATING DEPARTMENT. HIS FATHER RETIRED FROM THE UNITED STATES FORCE AIR IN 1984. BOBBY'S MOTHER KATE BROWN JONES WAS A PRESCHOOL TEACHER FOR ALMOST 20 YEARS IN FORT WORTH, TEXAS AT GENSIS UNITED METHODIST CHURCH.

FAMILY STORY HAS IT THAT THE OAK TREES PLANTED EAST OF THE CHURCH BUILDING WERE DEDICATED TO THE MEMORY OF HIS PATERNAL GRANDMOTHER BONNIE THELMA TURCOTTE JONES.

THIS COLORING BOOK IS DEDICATED TO THE LOVING MEMORY OF BOBBY'S MATERNAL GRANDMOTHER SUE MORRISON BROWN. JONES SPENT MANY SUMMERS AT HIS GRANDMOTHER'S FARM IN LUBBOCK, TEXAS. HE LOVED THAT FARM. HE WOULD GO EXPLORING AROUND THE COTTON FIELDS THAT SURROUNDED HIS GRANDMOTHER'S FARM.

BEFORE THE COTTON FIELDS, JONES' AUNT MARGARET BROWN JOHNSTON AND HIS COUSINS GREW AND SOLD VEGETABLES DURING THE SUMMER. HIS FAMILY AND HIS RELATIVES PICKED CORN, SQUASH, BLACK EYED PEAS, CUCUMBERS, AND ZUCCHINI. HE LOVED SHELLING BLACK EYED PEAS. HE REMEMBERS THAT HIS FAMILY AND RELATIVES WOULD HAVE A CONTEST ABOUT WHO COULD SHELL THE MOST BLACK EYED PEAS OR WHO COULD SHUCK THE MOST EARS OF CORN.

BOBBY REMEMBERS HIS MATERNAL GRANDMOTHER, HIS MOM, AND HIS AUNTS CANNING AND FREEZING VEGETABLES. HE WAS VERY AMAZED AT HOW HIS GRANDMOTHER, HIS AUNTS, AND HIS MOM WORKED LIKE A WELL OILED MACHINE TO GET THIS PROJECT DONE. HE WOULD SIT AND WATCH THEM WORK LIKE A TEAM CANNING AND FREEZING VEGETABLES. HE WAS IN AWE.

HE LOVED SPENDING TIME WITH HIS MATERNAL GRANDMOTHER. SHE WAS A REMARKABLE WOMAN. HE WISHES THAT HIS FRIENDS AND THE GENERATION IN HIS FAMILY AFTER HIS GENERATION COULD HAVE KNOWN THEIR GREAT GRANDMOTHER BROWN. SHE WAS SO FULL OF LIFE

AND LOVE. SHE ACCOMPLISHED SO MANY THINGS DURING HER TIME. JONES HAS HIS MATERNAL GRANDMOTHER'S DIPLOMA FROM TEXAS TECHNOLOGICAL COLLEGE (TEXAS TECH UNIVERSITY) FROM 1932. IT IS A REMINDER THAT ONCE A PERSON PUTS THEIR MIND TO ACCOMPLISHING THINGS IN LIFE. IT CAN BE ACHIEVED. STICK WITH IT AND KEEP MOVING FORWARD !!!

JONES GRADUATED FROM SOUTHWEST HIGH SCHOOL IN FORT WORTH, TEXAS IN 1985. HE ATTENDED TEXAS TECH UNIVERSITY IN LUBBOCK, TEXAS AND GRADUATED IN 1989 WITH A BFA IN ART (PAINTING AND DRAWING). THEN BOBBY ATTENDED THE UNIVERSITY OF NEW MEXICO IN ALBUQUERQUE, NEW MEXICO AND OBTAINED A M.A. IN ART EDUCATION (MUSEUM EDUCATION, CERAMICS, AND PHOTOGRAPHY) 1994. JONES GRADUATED FROM CENTRAL NEW MEXICO COMMUNITY COLLEGE IN 2014 WITH AN ALTERNATIVE TEACHING DEGREE IN SPECIAL EDUCATION.

WHILE ATTENDING TEXAS TECH UNIVERSITY, BOBBY BECAME A LIFE MEMBER OF BETA SIGMA'S ALPHA PHI OMEGA AND A MEMBER OF GOLDEN KEY NATIONAL HONOR SOCIETY. HE IS A TEXAS TECH LEGACY! WHILE AT CNM, JONES WAS INDUCTED INTO PHI THETA KAPPA HONOR SOCIETY IN 2013.

BOBBY STARTED WORKING FOR ALBUQUERQUE PUBLIC SCHOOLS IN 2014. HE HAS PLANS TO BECOME A TEACHER IN NEW MEXICO. HE HAS EXHIBITED HIS ARTWORK IN ALBUQUERQUE, NEW MEXICO AT THE FACTORY ON 5TH, THE 606 ART GALLERY, THE TORTRUGA GALLERY, AND FIRST UNITARIAN CHURCH'S SOCIAL HALL IN THE ALL MEMBER ART EXHIBIT. JONES HAS MANY ART PROJECTS IN THE MAKING AT THIS TIME. IT WILL BE EXCITING TO SEE THEM COME TO LIFE!

New Mexico Dreamscapes II

MY LABORATORY   MY PROCEDURE MANUAL
AUTHOR SIGNATURE FORM

Name of book	How to be a Lab Director 2019 edition		
Author of Book	Philip A. Dauterman, MD PMB 276 P.O. Box 10001 Saipan, MP 96950 E-mail: drp_dauterman@yahoo.com	Board Certified in Anatomic Pathology and Clinical Pathology	Since 1996
Mandatory Comment Field	In my Pathology training days, the program strongly favored Anatomic Pathology. The Clinical Pathology training was the minimum number of months to be eligible for boards, and all classroom work. There was not even a single "hands on" course that involved on-the-job training in a real life setting. After graduation, I had a great deal of classroom knowledge, but did not know how to deal with real-life situations in real labs. I learned that on the fly and on the job. America's Pathology training programs still strongly emphasize Anatomic Pathology at the expense of Clinical Pathology. To date, there has not been an educational book written about how to be a hospital Lab Director. This book is intended to fill that void.		
Optional comment field			
Owner of book		Note: if the book ownership changes, strike the former book owner's name and affiliation with a single line and write in the new book owner's name and affiliation. All changes must be signed and dated. Use of white-out is prohibited.	
Affiliation of owner of book			
Author signature	*Philip A. Dauterman, M.D.*	**Sixth edition published Jan. 1, 2019**	

How to be a Lab Director 2019 edition by Philip A. Dauterman, MD
with graphs by Steven Matthew R. Dauterman
Table of Contents

Chapter 1 – Intro to the Clinical Lab

Chapter 2 – Things you probably don't need to know as a Lab Director
    A. The color on the top of the drawing tubes.
    B. Diagnostic precision and accuracy
    C. Sensitivity and specificity
    D. Limit of detection and limit of quantitation

Chapter 3 – How to read a Levey-Jennings chart

Chapter 4 – Pick your Westgard rules carefully

Chapter 5 – Proficiency testing and corrective actions

Chapter 6 – What to do if one analyte fails 2 or more proficiency testing events in one year

Chapter 7 – How to put a new analyzer into service
    A. Pick which equipment you want to buy
    B. Decide to rent, buy or lease the equipment
    C. The new analyzer and the Service Rep arrive
    D. Check correlation
    E. Do calibration, verification of calibration and check linearity
    F. Set the Analytical Measurement Range (AMR), Reference Range and Critical Values
    G. Write the procedures for the new equipment
    H. Controls, final preparations, going live with the new analyzer and retiring the old analyzer

Chapter 8 – How to put a new test onto an existing analyzer

Chapter 9 – How to deal with analyzer breakdowns

Chapter 10 – How to read a linearity proficiency test report

Chapter 11 – How to write a policy and/or procedure

Chapter 12 – Quality Assurance, complaints, incident reports and root cause analysis

Chapter 13 – How to deal with personnel problems
    A. How to spot a potentially homicidal employee
    B. How to spot a potentially suicidal employee
    C. How to deal with 2 lab employees that do not get along
    D. How to deal with a disagreement between employees inside and outside lab
    E. How to deal with the chronically late to work employee
    F. How to deal with an employee with performance and/or behavioral issues

Chapter 14 – Physician and administrator demands on lab and physician ordering practices